# Parents in Control

# DAVID RICE

**HARVEST HOUSE PUBLISHERS**
Eugene, Oregon 97402

**PARENTS IN CONTROL**

Copyright © 1987 by Harvest House Publishers
Eugene, Oregon 97402

Library of Congress Catalog Card Number 86-080706
ISBN 0-89081-505-4

# CONTENTS

# Parents in Control

# 1

# Parents Out of Control

One of my favorite bumper stickers reads, "Insanity is hereditary—you get it from your kids." That's what Barbara and Jim could easily have said when they visited my office for the first time. You see, they had been victimized by one of life's cruelest jokes: Their oldest son had just become a junior higher! He was challenging them at every turn, refusing to do household chores, terrorizing his younger brother and sister, and constantly making the most creative mouth noises known to mankind. Mom would get enraged like a rabid dog while Dad would retreat to his study and lock the door. "We don't know what to do with him," Barbara sighed. "He's changed overnight! And we don't like what we see. What have we done wrong?"

"I don't think you've done anything wrong to create this," I replied. "You have just entered man's final frontier, adolescence! There are several key things you need to know and do, and we can work on these together to make your journey through teenagehood more pleasurable. You can get back in control."

Every parent feels a bit insane and out of control from time to time. It's normal to have thoughts like "Why did God let me have kids?" or "Is there a 24-hour day-care place somewhere?" or "We weren't crazy before we had children, were we?"

Once we have children, life is never the same. Of course, we all have to learn that for ourselves. When my wife, Kim, and I were first married, we vowed never to let children get in the way of our marriage. Yet years later as Kim was eating her umpteenth hamburger at the local fast-food stand, I suggested that on Saturday night we leave the kids home and paint the town. When the big date came, I asked Kim where she would enjoy going for dinner. With a slight grin she said, "Anyplace where I don't have to unwrap my food!" That's when I realized we had lost control.

Kids do seem to control us. They have perfected a variety of clever, disgusting, annoying behaviors designed to drive parents up the wall! In fact, I would wager that most preschool curricula contain courses designed to torment and frustrate parents:

Persistency 101: 50 creative ways to ask for a bedtime drink of water.

Art 105: How to create wall designs with spaghetti sauce.

Social Ecology 108: Getting out of chores by claiming "How come my little sister doesn't have to do it?"

Psychology 100: Last-minute tantrums for the grocery store line.

It takes years to learn how to overcome such programming. Then, just when we think we have parenting down pat, the teenage years explode upon us! All that once seemed to work now goes out the window. Children that were once affectionate, sensible, compliant, and thoughtful now change into larger-than-life gremlins. It's at this stage that parents feel most out of control. In fact, they are! Teenagers are, by definition, difficult to control.

If you spent any time around a group of parents with teenage kids, you might hear them grumbling about how:

Kathy, 13, stays in her room, shutting out the family. The paramedics arrive to insure that she is not becoming mummified.
Tom, 16, stays out until all hours of the night, ignoring the curfew. "What curfew?" he innocently asks as he drags in when the morning paper arrives.

Sarah, 15, forgets to feed the cat. Only when the cat begins to look anorexic do the parents get the message.

Jim, 14, unloads only half the dishwasher. Unfortunately, he puts dirty dishes back in to replace the half he unloaded. After all, didn't Mom say, "Put the dishes away"?

Kevin, 12, is impossible to get into bed. What's worse, in his later teen years he will be impossible to get out of bed.

As if the behavior is not enough, the struggles of parenthood are compounded by such nagging thoughts as:

"I am the worst parent on the block."

"My son will turn out rotten. I will have produced the world's most rotten kid."

"I have failed. It's my fault. No one else is responsible for my child's behavior, not even my child."

"My child doesn't love me. In fact, he named his dart board after me."

"My daughter has won and the Battle of Armageddon is over."

"My mom was right: God is punishing me for my childhood behaviors."

Parents try all kinds of tactics to regain control. Every book on parenting is read cover to cover, underlined, and marked in four colors. Seminars are attended with the fervency of a starved dog. Talk shows are on 24 hours a day, causing weakened fingers from frantic knob-turning. As a result, desperate strong-arm techniques are usually the first shot:

> "All right, you're grounded until you're 30."
> "No dinner for you for 40 nights and 40 days."
> "You'll see who's in charge; I'll take your MasterCard away from you!"

When those threats fail, creative and exotic rewards are tried:

> "If you clean up your room I'll give you a car."
> "Eat your peas and you can spend the night at Baskin-Robbins."
> "When you finish your homework I'll let you talk on the phone for three hours."

When all else fails, there is one last ace in the hole that parents feel might possibly work: *guilt.* Parents use and reuse phrases handed down from their ancestors to coerce children into proper behavior:

> "You don't know what you're doing to your mom. She'll die of a rare tropical disease if you don't stop!"
> "I can't believe you! I've done so much for you and this is what I get! After all, I'm the one that gave you birth! Don't you remember?"

"Son, when I was _____, I used to walk
_____ miles to school in the _____. My parents could not afford much, so I lived without
_____. But I appreciated all that I had!"

All of this makes an extremely painful situation for a parent. It's distressing to feel angry, worried, guilty, and humiliated over parenting situations that seem beyond help. It's even worse to feel out of control!

## PARENTING AND STRESS

Parenting is the toughest job in the world—just ask any parent. If you saw an ad in the newspaper for an opening in this position, it might look something like this:

**WANTED**: for full-time, 24-hours-a-day, 7--days-a-week, 12-months-a-year, 18-to-30-year parenting position. **No experience required.** Training provided on the job with little or no instruction. No owner's manual; little if any staff support. **Job description:** refereeing, cleaning, cooking, chauffeuring, entertaining, wrestling; must be willing to hand out money on demand; must be able to work part-time job to supplement income. **Benefits:** development of fruits of the Spirit: love, joy, peace, patience, etc. If interested, check in at any household. **Opening:** immediate!

When I stop and think about it, I received more

instruction and training in operating my computer than I ever did in becoming a parent. No wonder so many of us parents have felt out of control! It is true on-the-job training.

What contributes to the stress that parents feel today? I am convinced that part of the answer lies in the fact that nothing seems permanent. Ideas, products, and philosophies seem to change daily. What worked when we were children went out with the Ice Age, or at least that's what our kids tell us. During the last 40 years our society has undergone more change than in any other period of history.

Just look at the number of books on parenting. A new one comes out every day. If you were to buy only a quarter of what's available, it would cost more than 5,000 dollars! And that doesn't include seminars, tapes, and film series. No wonder we feel out of control: Look at the amount of advice!

Perhaps you're wondering who to believe. For example, what do I have to say that's significantly different from all the other books on parenting? What you'll find offered in these pages is a straightforward plan to regain control of your children. My message is simple: *Know what behaviors you want, state the rules clearly and precisely, follow through with a plan, and be consistent.* By the time you are through reading this book, you will be able to implement a model that will guide you in retaking control of every behavior you wish to change in your children. The key is how hard you are willing to work at it.

Parents also feel out of control because of stress. Marital and financial insecurities, poor health, caring for aged parents, and job changes are just a few of the pressures that we face. Life feels like a big balancing act as we try to juggle the stresses and demands of living with personal fulfillment, while at the same time providing for the emotional needs of the family. The result of stress is self-absorption, and the result of self-absorption is neglect of the family.

Consider single mothers trying to support themselves and raise several children. Most of such mothers are working full-time while their children are in day-care centers. Many of these moms receive little or no financial support from their ex-husbands, and these women are concerned about finances, the welfare of their children, their future as a single person, dating, and job security. No wonder they have little strength or enthusiasm left over for parenting—so much energy is spent just surviving day to day!

Or consider the plight of the unhappy marriage. Typically, first-time marriages last about seven years. Much of that time is spent by one spouse trying to get the other involved in the relationship, in parenting, and in church. When the more interested spouse begins to feel resentful, hurt, and angry, his or her emotional energy gets invested in the children. That's a heavy load for a child to carry—making up for what's lacking in the marriage. As a result, parenting becomes off-balance and out of control.

## TYPES OF OUT-OF-CONTROL PARENTS

Regaining control of your kids starts by realizing where you are out of control. The Johnson family got the message loud and clear from a surprising source.

The tension in my office was so thick you could cut it with a knife. On one side of the room was the mother, Barbara, and the father, Jim. Opposite them, as far away as possible, were 16-year-old Darryl and his younger brother and sister.

"What is the problem that brings you here?" I asked the parents.

"The constant fighting between Darryl and his brother and sister," replied Jim. "It never stops. He picks on them night and day. Then I get into it."

"And that makes it worse," Barbara interrupted. "Then the real yelling and screaming begins."

"Well, you never help!" Jim snapped back. "You always side with Darryl and let him get away with murder!"

"You know what your problem is?" screamed the 16-year-old boy. "You can't control us!" The parents sat stunned. "Dad, you are never home. And when you are, all you do is tell us what to do. Both you and Mom fight all the time because you can't agree on what to do."

They could never have heard the truth more clearly. Darryl was right: The parents were out of control. They couldn't agree on how to handle the kids, and in their anger they yelled at each other.

In my years of private practice as a psychologist and family counselor, I have witnessed hundreds of out-of-control families. Among these families in trouble I've noticed several parenting styles. As we examine these styles, see if one or more describes your own parenting methods. Each style has a brief description, the resulting behavior of the kids, and some questions to help you evaluate if you fit that style.

## The Divide-and-Conquer Parents

Children love to get what they want, and they have a myriad of tactics to achieve their goals. They've learned that when one parent says no, the other one is sure to say yes. The trouble is that neither parent knows what the other has said. The child gets his wish, and Mom and Dad are at each other's throat!

"You always give in!" exclaims one parent. "You're too easy on them."

"You never let them do anything!" snorts the other. "You don't let them have any fun!"

That's all a child needs to hear. The battle is won!

*The result:* children who manipulate authority and cannot accept a "No" without a challenge; they believe that rules are made to be bent or ignored.

*Questions for you:* Do you remember pitting your parents against each other? Do your kids favor asking one parent over the other? Which parent says no more often? Are fights with your spouse often about a lack of communication in decision-making, or not supporting the other's ideas and decisions?

## The Parent's Parent

More common in single-parent households, this child is parent to the parent. His concern is where Mom is, how much food is in the house, who Mom is dating, keeping the younger siblings corralled, and making sure the house is in order. When a child is responsible, it is very easy for parents to hand over some parenting duties. While sharing the duties of household chores is an integral part of family life, the problem arises when this "parental" child, usually the oldest, wants to be a child and to abdicate some of his parental duties.

"I have so little time for myself," 17-year-old Sharon sighed as she slumped down in my office sofa. "As soon as I get home from school I have to watch my brother and sister, do the laundry, and try to get dinner ready. I know Mom works hard, but she expects me to do a lot of her work for her. Sometimes I feel like the parent, except I don't get the respect!"

"I'll bet that's part of why you've been so angry the past few months," I suggested. "You almost don't have a life of your own."

"Yeah, that's what it feels like. It makes me want to run away."

*The result:* a child who is prematurely an adult; most of the younger years are spent performing adult duties. This child is unable to have fun, or even stop and relax, without feeling guilty.

*Questions for you:* Who was the responsible one in your family when you were a child? Do you find your oldest child complaining about too much work? Have you found yourself relying more and more on the kids to help pull the load? Are your kids spending more time doing chores than being with you? Do your kids play as much as they used to?

## The Yo-Yo Parents

This style is governed by the parents' moods. When things are smooth, Mom and Dad are lax; when things are getting out of control, the parents resort to making up a new list of the Ten Commandments. For the kids, it's like playing checkers with someone who keeps changing the rules!

As 14-year-old Jim said to me, "I poke my head out in the morning to see what mood they're in. Then I know what they'll get on me about and what they won't."

"So you can't really count on anything being the same around home," I said.

"No. I hate having them change the rules all the time, or else say it's a rule when they've never told me about it. I get busted for stuff I didn't even know about."

*The result:* children who grow up with a sense of unpredictability in their lives; nothing can be counted on to be consistent. In fact, these children often hold back, taking few risks in life until they see what others are doing.

*Questions for you:* Were your parents consistent in their discipline? Did they follow through on enforcing rules and limits? Do you find yourself saying "Go ahead, it's not worth the hassle" and then getting angry the next day for that decision? Do your kids seem cautious in asking you for things, waiting to see what your mood is? Do they complain that you change your mind too much or don't tell them what you want and when?

## The Squeaky-Clean Parents

These parents always have a better way of doing things. They either reject what their kids do or criticize how they do it. Most often these parents feel they are instructing their children in how to improve and achieve greater goals. They think that if they encourage and support their kids too much, they'll become complacent and never achieve anything worthwhile.

"Well, son, what about this C?" the father said in a judgmental tone.

"I did get three B's and two A's! That's pretty good!" replied his son.

"Yes, but what about the C?" the dad snapped back.

Sadly, these children react with feelings of inadequacy and are unable to enjoy life. Either they take things too seriously or they don't try at all.

*The result:* children who constantly feel frustrated, angry, and guilty. "I will never achieve enough to please my parents," they think. These young people grow up with a constant need to prove and re-prove themselves each and every day.

*Questions for you:* Did your parents support and encourage you? Do you live with a nagging feeling that what you did was not good enough? Do your children play it safe and take few risks, or get angry and frustrated when they lose?

## The Nothing-Is-Too-Good-for-My-Child Parents

These parents raise the well-known spoiled brat. If there are any rules, they are only suggestions or advice; rarely is anything enforced. After all, children never have to be disciplined or corrected for what is not specifically told them. It looks like an easy out for parents!

In reality these parents are afraid of hurting the child or making him angry if they set limits. They don't want him to feel unloved. After all, doesn't abundant love make discipline unnecessary?

*The result:* children who grow up without learning what is generally considered right and wrong behavior. They have little discipline, patience, or social skills. They are unable to set limits for themselves and often leave jobs or tasks unfinished. The phrases often heard by kids of permissive parents are "Why should I?" and "What's in it for me?"

*Questions for you:* Do your kids start projects and chores, then leave them unfinished? Are you afraid that if you discipline your child you will be perceived as unloving and harsh? Do your kids have angry outbursts and temper tantrums when you don't give in initially to their demands?

## The Gestapo Parents

These parents require absolute conformity. Control of the family is through adherence to a set of standards that only changes once per decade. The thoughts and opinions of young people are not allowed. "If I want your opinion, I'll ask for it" is a phrase often heard by these overcontrolling parents.

"Gestapo Parents" have a difficult time with anyone's opinions that differ from their own. They feel challenged each time one of their children says anything different. These families talk very little to each other. Why should they? Nothing is worth saying unless it agrees with government policy.

*The result:* children who become very conforming and conservative but have a difficult time thinking for themselves. Their feelings are not often expressed. People see them as detached and withdrawn or rigid and controlling. They often have quite a temper as well.

*Questions for you:* Which of your parents were you afraid of? Could you speak your mind freely when you were young? Do you find your kids saying that you don't listen to them? Is there a bolt of anger that shoots through you when the children or your spouse disagrees with you?

## The Mommy-and-Me Parents

This is the most frequent style among troubled families. It starts with a troubled marriage. Mom, to replace her failing relationship with Dad, becomes overly close to one or more of the kids. They become her (or his) confidant, crying pillow, therapist, and punching bag. With this type of burden, one of the kids eventually becomes both a problem and a "solution." The child's "acting-out" behavior at school, in the neighborhood, or at home becomes a cause of concern and is seen (unconsciously or consciously) as a solution to a troubled marriage. After all, it's difficult to focus on a strained marital relationship when one of the kids needs so much attention! In a strange way this seems to lessen the strain on the marriage for a time as the youngster becomes the focus of the family members.

Eight-year-old Jimmy was getting into trouble at school with his loud talking and joking in class. The problem commanded all of Mom and Dad's attention. He became the sole topic of their conversation and the focus of much of their energy. They met with the teacher, the principal, and the school psychologist. Little Jimmy was at the same time a *problem* to the parents and a *temporary solution* to their troubled marriage. In reality he was holding the marriage together. If Jimmy got better, guess what might happen?

*The result:* children who do not have lives of their own. They function as surrogate spouses, filling in the missing needs of Mom or Dad. These children get caught in the marital struggle, serving as pressure relief valves or emotional equals. Parents need them to be the best or most popular student, athlete, or musician. Even as they reach adulthood, the suction back into the marital mire cannot be escaped—they feel forced to give loyalty to one parent or the other.

*Questions for you:* Did your parents seem to confide more in you than in each other? Do you remember having to choose sides? Are your kids the central focus of conversations with your spouse? Is one of the kids constantly in trouble? Could he or she be what's keeping your marriage together? What would your marriage be like if your problem child suddenly got better?

## WHAT'S AHEAD

How do you match up? Do one or more of these styles describe your family? Well, cheer up. There is hope! You have just taken the first vital step to regaining control. Knowing what your parenting style is can begin to give you the freedom to change. As you read this book and experiment with the model I propose, you will be able to measure your progress against the style or styles with which you have just identified. When you look back, you'll be amazed at how far you have come!

But first you must do something that may sound strange. You actually cannot gain control of your family unless you . . . give up! That's right. This may sound crazy, but you'll understand as we examine a few popular myths that we tend to hold about parenting.

# 2

# Giving Up Before Going On

Kevin was a teenager who had never uttered a word in his entire life. His parents tried everything to get him to talk. They took him to speech and hearing specialists, who determined that there was no physiological reason why he could not speak. His parents took him to psychologists, who attempted to induce him to talk. Still no results. They tried motivating him through all kinds of incentives. But nothing worked.

One day when Kevin was 14 years old he came to the dinner table, sat down, and took a sip of soup. Suddenly he yelled, "This soup is cold!"

Astonished by her son's words, his mother blurted out, "You *can* talk! Why haven't you spoken before now? You know all the trouble we've gone through to get you to talk."

Kevin shrugged his shoulders and said, "Well, before now everything was okay."

Like Kevin's parents, all of us occasionally feel that our families are anything but normal. In fact, the question I'm most frequently asked by parents is, "Are we normal? Do other families have problems like ours?"

Our ideas of what is normal come from our own family experiences as well as from TV, books, school, our friends' families, seminars, talk shows, church leaders, and the backs of breakfast cereal boxes. The problem is that it's difficult to define what is normal. What works for Bill Cosby may not work for you!

Much of the trouble that families experience comes from what parents believe families ought to be like. Those "oughts," "shoulds," "musts," and "have to's" create pressure on people to fulfill unreal standards— standards that are not only unworkable but are impossible to attain. Statements such as "You must get grades as good as I did," "We ought to be happy at all times," or "My kids must appreciate all I do for them or I've failed as a parent" are examples. These "shoulds" and "oughts" become expectations which then evolve into demands, causing a family needless tension and frustration.

There is a name for these powerful beliefs: They are called "self-talk," things we tell ourselves that we come to believe as fact. It's important to understand such thinking because thoughts determine how we feel. In other words, our thoughts create our emotions. Proverbs 23:7 tells us that "as a man thinks in his heart, so is he" (KJV). When we believe that children should not get angry with their parents, we will react with negative emotion the minute they do become angry. Our emotions respond to what we believe to be true, whether it is in fact true or not.

We need to ask ourselves "Is what we believe about children and family life true?" Parents often have "shoulds," "oughts," and "have to's" that are based on faulty thinking or irrational beliefs. Maybe that's why the members of your family don't always understand why you feel what you feel or do what you do. For that matter, maybe that's why you don't understand it either! *The New Mood Therapy* by David Burns and *Self Talk* by David Stoop are two good sources for you to read about changing faulty thinking.

Sometimes we're like the woman who, when she cooked ham, always cut off both ends before putting it in the pan. When asked by a neighbor why she did this, she replied, "That's what my mother always did." Curious, the neighbor went to the mother, asked the same question, and got the same reply. Finally she asked the grandmother, who answered "The ham was too large for my pan, so I had to cut off both ends." It's easy to hold onto myths; they seem to have a life of their own because we don't understand where they come from. Once we identify our personal myths (many of which are built on faulty thinking and shaky logic), we can give them up and move on to gaining more control in our emotional and family life.

Here are several common myths. See if you can identify with one or more of them from your own childhood as well as in your present family.

*Myth 1: My family should be perfect.*

One of the most difficult things for families to do is seek counseling. We want to think our home is perfect and without problems. Actually, the idea of the typical, happy family is becoming a thing of the past. With the divorce rate hovering around 50 percent, increasing numbers of people will live in single-parent households. Should these parents feel like failures because they aren't part of the American dream? Of course not! But unfortunately too many feel just that way.

Other families with a learning-disabled child, a teenager abusing alcohol or drugs, or experiencing marital conflicts or serious illnesses, feel alone in their "badness" and in their pain. Yet I wonder if the perfect American family ever existed. As I sit with family after family in counseling, I observe how we all are much more alike than different. The issues I struggle with in my own home are reflected to a degree in every family I counsel. In fact, I often learn as much from families I counsel as they learn from me.

One young couple sat across from me visibly shaken as they recounted the exploits of their five-year-old son. He would get out of bed several times each night, wake up early and demand breakfast, refuse to come home for dinner when told, and scream and throw fits in the grocery store checkout line. They were here to see me because they felt out of control.

"Dave," the young mother said, "I'll bet you don't have problems like this with your kids. After all, you are a psychologist. You're trained to handle things like this."

I couldn't help but laugh as I answered, "Sometimes I think that's more of a problem than an asset. In fact, sometimes my wife will poke me in the ribs and say, 'You're the psychologist; you figure it out!' We all have problems with parenting, and I'm certainly no exception."

If you struggle to be *perfect* parents, it may be because of your family background. Could your parents admit mistakes and allow you to do the same? The ability to admit wrongdoing, take responsibility for it, and apologize creates an atmosphere of acceptance and understanding. People who are willing to take risks and forge ahead know that errors are just that—errors, not statements of inadequacy. One of the statements I hear most often from teenagers is, "My dad (or mom) never admits he made a mistake. He will never say he was wrong."

One couple came to see me about their daughter, yet the father felt, "We *should* be able to work this out at home."

"Do you two talk at home about this problem with Cindy?" I asked.

"Well, no," he replied. "But we should be able to."

"Should be able to?"

"Well, yes."

"It doesn't sound like that's happening. What prevents the family from talking about problems together?"

"We always end up yelling," the daughter jumped in. "We can never talk!"

In this family, the father's adamant idea that "we should be able to work all things out" was keeping everyone on edge. They were unable to share their thoughts and feelings without feeling the pressure to "do it right." The more they tried to get together, the worse the problem became.

The only solution is to admit it when you are wrong. Give up the myth of perfection. Let your spouse or children know if you have placed unneeded pressure on them to be like the Cosby family. As you allow yourself the freedom to take risks and make mistakes, your family members will begin to do the same.

It is also essential to realize that whatever is causing hurt, anger, fear, or sadness is being experienced by thousands of families *right now*. You are not alone. That is the message of such groups as Alcoholics Anonymous, Families Anonymous, Tough Love, and other support groups designed to give people the feeling that "we're all in this together." When we give up the myth of the perfect family, stop denying that we have problems to work through, and deal with our conflicts in a spirit of patience, compassion and understanding, then psychological growth begins to take place.

*Myth 2: Children should appreciate and verbalize all that their parents do for them.*

"I can't believe it," sighed an exasperated father. "I gave John the skateboard we promised him, let him watch more television, and raised his allowance. Yet he still wants more! You'd think he was the King of England. He just takes and takes and all I get is a grunt, if that. I want to quit!"

Sound familiar? Parenting is, in some ways, a thankless job. Signs of obvious appreciation are few and far between. Some parents feel that what they give up and sacrifice for the sake of the kids *must* be recognized, eulogized, and immortalized. We want to know that what we do (and don't get to do) is noticed and appreciated. Of course the retort uttered by older children, especially teens, in response to their parents' plea for appreciation is "I didn't ask to be born!"

Expecting and demanding appreciation places a heavy burden on the child. He or she is expected to give back what we put in, to demonstrate that our sacrifice is worth it. One mother, upon finding that her 12-year-old son had a slight learning disability, was tremendously relieved. She felt that his poor school performance was her fault, the result of inadequate parenting. It's as if his behavior was a direct statement about her abilities as a parent. Yet in reality our children's behavior is a result of a number of factors.

It's natural for parents to look to their children for recognition as "good enough" providers, nurturers, role models, and leaders. It's sometimes difficult to know how we are doing, since there is so little feedback that can tell us if we are on the right track or not. When the self-esteem of a mother or father is low, children are seen as a mirror that can reflect a positive self-image back to the parent. Children are expected to act only in ways that "reflect" this good self—"my son the ball player," "my daughter the actress." Certainly it's good to encourage our children to do their best, but do their best for *whom*? They can never make up for what's lacking in us, and they shouldn't have to.

At this point we often find that what we do for our children is not appreciated. We can react with feelings of hurt, anger, resentment, sadness, and even depression. As a result, we hold back emotionally and physically from our kids or get angry with them when they don't do what we ask because we have just done something for them. Or else we try to do even more, as if we didn't already do enough. Yet they can never give back in proportion to what we give.

Jesus must have felt a twinge of hurt when He healed the ten lepers and only one returned to thank Him. Yet He did not demand that they come back, nor did He stop healing people. He understood that giving does not have a price tag. As parents, this needs to be our attitude. Our children do say "thank you" in many subtle ways—with a hug or a smile, by asking us to play ball with them, or by giving us their best effort in washing the car. Our reward comes through our involvement in their lives as they grow and mature into young men and women.

To give up Myth Number 2, start by looking at your feelings when your children disappoint you. Do you get angry with them? Perhaps you feel cheated or hurt. If so, examine your behavior when you have these feelings. Do you withdraw emotionally, becoming silent, sad, or sullen as if to punish them for their lack of thankfulness? Or do you turn on the juice and try to do even more, thinking you haven't done enough? Do you perhaps get angry when they don't take out the trash, thinking they should do so because you just drove them to the beach? It's much better to tell them it hurts when you don't receive a "thank you," and keep it at that. Don't drag in all you do for them and all they don't do for you—that's another issue. Your kids need to know that you have feelings too. Don't pull away, turn on the juice, or attack. Be honest, share your feelings, and tell them what you want.

Being a parent is to be a perpetual student of human personality . . . yours and your children's. We learn along with our kids, don't we? So instead of expecting and demanding gratitude from them, let's look at parenting as a long-term investment with an eternal return. The dividends are slow in coming, but after all, this is a long-term growth fund!

*Myth 3: Children should not get angry at their parents, and parents should not get angry at their children.*

If we were to take a poll of counselors and psychologists, I'm sure we would find that one of the top problems for which people seek help is anger. They are either too angry or are unable to express their anger. Some families have so much anger that children constantly feel the home will split apart anytime a fight breaks out. Other families pride themselves for never having an angry word, but this doesn't mean that they don't have anger; it just means that it's suppressed.

One young man was brought to me because he ran away whenever he felt angry. He would leave the house and be gone for hours. The parents felt he was being too rebellious, and shouldn't be allowed to be angry at them.

"My parents won't let me say anything about how I feel," 13-year-old Michael explained, "especially if I don't agree with them. My dad says I can't say a word back. It's like they don't care what I want."

"So what do you do when you feel angry?" I asked.

"I yell and then go and ride my skateboard. When I cool off I come back."

"How do your parents react to this?" I asked.

"It makes them mad. They say I shouldn't run away like that. But when I'm angry, what am I supposed to do—put my fist through the wall?"

Parents like Michael's feel that any difference of opinion with their children is a challenge to their authority. "You must not disagree with us" is an underlying theme (myth) in many households. "And if you do," they say, "we don't want to hear about it."

What hangs us up about anger? Some of us feel that if we express anger there will be retaliation. We will get punished by people withdrawing, attacking, or quietly plotting a reprisal against us. So a fear of what will happen in return keeps some of us from letting others know how we feel.

Another hang-up is that we think we have no right to be angry. So instead we swallow our feelings and pretend that everything is fine. The anger builds like a pressure cooker with no release valve: Eventually it explodes or gets "buried alive," only to surface as deep resentment months or years later. In raising children, this can make a parent timid, permissive, passive, or unpredictable, resulting in tremendous feelings of loss of control.

How was anger expressed in your family when you were a child? Was Mom quiet and Dad loud, or just the reverse? How did you express anger as a child? Were you punished for your feelings of anger? In what ways do your children express their discontent with you now? Do you allow them to say they are angry or allow yourself to let them know you are angry?

When you are angry, tell it! But put it in "I" messages such as "I feel angry right now" or "When you don't put the trash cans away when I ask you to I feel angry and frustrated." Don't impose blame with phrases like "You never do what I say" or "Why can't you do such a little thing for me? After all, I just spent a ton of money on your skateboard!" Keep it simple. Tell your feelings and state what you want.

If your anger feels out of control, cool off. Say something like "I'm really angry right now, and I can't think clearly. We'll talk about this when I cool off a bit." Then make sure that you do talk later!

*Myth 4: There's one bad egg in every nest.*

Like it or not, it's impossible to approve of everything your children did, do, and will do. There are even times when we don't like who they are. Yet we try, with God's grace and compassion, to love them as Christ loves us— unconditionally, without regard to whether they have earned it or not. The problem is that most of us have never experienced a love like this, so how can we give what we have never experienced?

One frustrated mother said about her 14-year-old daughter, "We've had problems with her ever since I can remember. Yet her older sister has never given us a bit of trouble. We are doing the same things, so why doesn't anything seem to work anymore?"

"How are your daughters different?" I asked.

"Oh, it's like night and day. The younger one is so much more outgoing, loud, emotional, and energetic."

"And that's what leaves you confused. What works with the older, quiet sister won't always work with your youngest. You need to accept and enjoy these differences. Don't resent them, or else your daughter will feel your pressure to be like her big sister. That will make things worse, not better."

It would be so easy to "carbon copy" our parenting style from one child to the next, but it doesn't work that way. Personality studies of birth order have shown that differences are both inevitable and impossible to overlook. When you stop to think about it, how boring and stale life would be if all the children in your family were "clones" of each other!

As a result of believing that all our children should act the same and be treated equally, families frequently single out a "problem child." "We are here to 'fix' him or her," they say in so many words when they visit my counseling office. Frankly, the child *is* a problem, yet the label of "the bad egg" can eventually become the bigger issue. The child misbehaves and acts out, the parents react, the child acts out even more, and the parents react once again, perpetuating a vicious, escalating cycle. It's like a merry-go-round that never stops.

Often when a child exhibits problem behavior, he is singled out in the family as a special source of concern for the parents. A child might have any variety of symptoms, such as bed-wetting, lying, fighting, or stealing, but whatever the difficulties of the child, the disturbed behavior keeps the parents involved in attempting to help him and to change his behavior. What they don't realize is that the "problem child" may be reacting to being treated like the other children in the family. His misbehavior could be a way of saying, "Let me be different. Don't expect me to be like my big brother."

Unfortunately, the feeling that a child gets of being the "problem" becomes a self-fulfilling prophecy. He begins to anticipate getting into trouble. After all, he always has! So the merry-go-round continues.

Do you have a child whom you call your "problem child?" Are you spending more time getting angry with one of your kids while the others seem to be doing all right? What is it that your child's misbehavior might be communicating to you?

To change this situation, look at how your behavior might be feeding the vicious cycle. Do your statements indicate blame, causing your child to feel more inadequate and thus misbehave even more? Is your response to his misbehavior working? Then why keep doing it? Get all the help you can, whether professional or otherwise, to enable you to pull back and look at the merry-go-round your family is riding. This could be one of the most important steps you will ever take!

*Myth 5: All teenagers who rebel are abnormal.*

One exasperated parent told me, "I wouldn't have believed it if I hadn't seen it myself! My daughter seemed to change overnight. It's as if the first day of junior high put a spell on her. She won't talk to us anymore. She doesn't want to be seen with us and shuts herself up in her room. Getting her to go out with the family is like pulling teeth. You'd think we have the plague or something!"

Adolescence is a time of many changes—physical, emotional, spiritual, intellectual, and social. According to famous psychologist Erik Erikson, children between the ages of 11 or 12 up through 22 or 23 pull away from the family unit and try to establish an identity of their own. This is what parents often call "rebellion." Actually, as a psychologist, I worry about the kids who *don't* rebel rather than the ones who do. Like trying on several hats to see what fits, teenagers "try on" new identities. Many of these "hats" scare parents to death, yet the teenagers *must* try them on. Those teens who don't challenge parents in any way grow up without a sense of values—values that have been tested and found to be true, like purifying metal in a blazing hot furnace.

Teens rebel (try on new hats) in a variety of ways. You say "white," they say "black"; you say "stop," they say "go." Music, clothes, fads, sports, food, guys, girls, cars, and the like are hats that seem to go with every teen in one way or another—and against every parent. Each interest seems to be the one they'll have for life, even though it lasts only a day, a week, or a few months. The once levelheaded youngster now gets lost in whatever is the hot item at the moment.

Young people also begin to think differently, often becoming very critical and argumentative. Mom is now the worst Mom on the planet, not like the "other" Moms, who all seem to understand a lot more about teenagers. Teens seem to believe that there is an ideal parent out there somewhere, and it's not you or I!

In addition, their thinking is more self-centered, as if the universe revolves around them. They feel like they're the topic of everyone's thoughts: "You and Dad always talk about me behind my back" (translation: "I need to know I'm important enough to be talked about"). It's like they're saying, "I want to be noticed by everyone, but just don't say anything bad about me." Or it's like the youngster who, when asked by his dad how his day went, says defensively, "Why?" as if any interest in him by his parents is part of an inquisition.

A result of these reactions is that parents feel as if every second with their teenager is a reenactment of "Star Wars." Yet the teenager's reactions are a normal part of development, a time of breaking away to establish a "me": once a child but now part child and part adult. Your children had a struggle to get out of the womb, and now, as teenagers, they fight in a similar fashion for a second birth—the birth of self.

What is the best way to respond to teenage rebellion? First of all, keep your ability to laugh. Almost without exception, parents who succeed with their teenagers have a sense of humor. These parents don't take themselves or their teenagers too seriously, and tend to see the trials and tribulations of adolescence as just that— an up-and-down time of life that will pass.

Second, be able to say no. As David Elkind says in his excellent book *All Grown Up And No Place To Go*, parents need to distinguish between what teenagers want and what they need. To be with friends is a need, but to stay out until all hours of the night is a want.

Third, listen. Kids like to talk. They need someone who can be a sounding board. As they try on new hats, they will ask you what they look like. Be honest, but *allow them the freedom to like it nonetheless*. Our fear is that they will like it for the rest of their lives. Your *attitude*, not your *agreement*, will determine whether they will continue to talk to you or not. Eating out, driving in the car, shooting baskets, shopping, watching TV, or working on a project are great times to talk *and* to listen. One mother said she learned more about her daughter by chauffeuring her and her friends around in the car than in any other way. It's pretty difficult not to hear what three chattering junior high girls are talking about in the backseat!

Fourth, nurture yourself and your relationships. Your marriage is first priority. I've seen many marriages suffer and finally break up during and after the teen years in a family. Studies have demonstrated that the teen years are one of the points of highest strain and lowest satisfaction in the marital relationship. If you're a single parent, you need support and encouragement all the more. Time for recreation, education, friendships, and spiritual growth is a *necessity*. I'm amazed at the number of couples I encounter in therapy who have not had a night away in months or a weekend alone in years. Your batteries must stay charged up! Having teens in the house can be as draining as leaving the headlights of your car on long after you have turned off the key. The engine must be started in order to recharge the battery!

*Myth 6: All children are the same and must be treated alike.*

Remember what it felt like the first time you held your first child, then your second, then your third? Or do you have so many children you've forgotten! If you think about it, each child had a different "feel" about him or her. One might have been fussy, another quiet, a third active and alert.

The problem is that many parents think all children are the same and should be treated alike. It's true that certain principles of discipline work for every child, but not all philosophies and strategies are appropriate. It does make parenting easier to use a "cookie cutter" approach to raising kids, but the reality is that each and every child is different. Research by Dr. Stella Chess and others has shown that each child has an individual behavioral style for responding to and coping with his environment. This style or temperament can be identified from early infancy. It has to do with how the child *behaves*, not his ability. Two children may be able to dress themselves properly or ride a bike with equal skill, yet they may differ in the quickness with which they move or the ease in which they enter a social situation.

Dr. Chess has identified three temperamental types or patterns from the many studies on individual differences in infants and children. The first type is the *difficult child*. No doubt you are thinking to yourself, "I have at least one of those!" These infants have irregular sleep and feeding patterns, slow acceptance of new foods, prolonged adjustment periods to new routines, and frequent and loud periods of crying. These babies and children are not easy to feed, put to sleep, bathe, or dress. New places, new activities, and strange faces may produce initial responses of loud protest or crying. These children make up about 10 percent of the total child population.

While counseling with the parents of a 16-year-old, the mother remarked that he was a tough baby to handle right off the bat. To this the boy remarked, "Yeah, you've said that so many times. You'll never let me forget it."

"Do you ever feel like the family would have been better off if you had never been born?" I asked.

"Oh, yes. I feel like I've been a pain to them all my life."

The problem of caring for and managing such a child can highlight a parent's reaction to stress. The same parents who are relaxed and consistent with an easy child may become resentful, guilty, or helpless with a difficult child. Like the boy I mentioned above, difficult children sense the resentful feelings of the parents, which then contribute further to the problem behavior. In turn, the increased acting out by the child makes the parents feel worse. On and on it goes until the cycle is broken through a change in the parents' attitudes and behavior, the maturing of the child, or family therapy.

By contrast, parents who do not feel guilty or put down by the difficult child's behavior may learn to enjoy the energy, the fight, and the strength of that infant or child. They see these qualities as potential assets, not liabilities.

The *easy child* is at the opposite end of the spectrum. This is the infant or child who is regular, responds positively to new situations, adapts quickly and easily to change, and shows a positive mood most of the time. These infants smile at strangers, sleep regularly, take to most new foods at once, adapt to school, and learn the rules of new games quickly. Naturally, these children develop significantly fewer behavior problems than do difficult infants.

The third type is the *slow-to-warm-up* child. Children with this pattern differ from the difficult infants in that their withdrawal from new things is quiet rather than loud. They usually do not have the irregularity of sleeping and eating functions, the frequent negative moods, and intense reactions of difficult infants. The mildly expressed withdrawal from new things is typically seen with the first bath, a new person, a stranger, a new place, or new food. The key issue in the development of slow-to-warm-up children is whether parents and teachers allow them to adapt at their own pace. Patience and encouragement are the best medicine for this pattern of child.

Each child is different, unique, and special in his or her own way. It takes understanding and patience with each one . . . some more than others. The difficult child takes strength, consistency, praise, and patience. The slow-to-warm-up child also requires patience, plus lots of instruction, time, and encouragement. The easy child needs all of these, except not in such abundant quantities.

Even though these three patterns have been identified, children in each pattern are still individually distinct. Each child needs individual attention, understanding, and encouragement in accord with his or her specific talents, gifts, shortcomings, and temperament. So let's learn to relax as parents and enjoy the uniqueness in each of our children!

Identifying the myths that we believe about parenting gives us the opportunity to look at our behavior with our children. How we react to our kids is based on our beliefs about children and child-rearing. If we believe that teenagers should not rebel or that all children are alike, then our parenting will reflect these ideas. When we recognize and begin to let go of these illogical myths, then we are able to look at new ideas. In the next chapter we will examine an approach to parenting that might be new to you. It's called "working your way out of a job!"

# 3

# Working Your Way Out of a Job

Imagine standing with your 16-year-old son on the busiest street corner in town. He is holding a suitcase stuffed with all the belongings needed to get started in life. You look at his sad and worried face and say, "It's time, Son. You're on your own. We have prepared you for life, and now the moment is right for you to leave us. You have our confidence and love. Keep in touch to let us know how you are. No matter what happens, though, you cannot come back home to live with us. This is it. Goodbye." You slowly turn and walk away as he stands motionless on the corner.

I have just put into human terms what animals do when the time has come to release their offspring into the world. Nature dramatically shows how parents tell their young they are ready to take on adult responsibilities. A mother bear senses the moment when she is to chase her two cubs up a tree and leave them stranded 20 feet high. She grunts as if to say "I love you," and then takes off into the woods. They are now on their own—no home-caught meals to go back to, no cave to borrow, no favorite tree to sack out in. That's it!

Mountain lions don't chase their young away when they're ready for adulthood. Instead, they growl, snap, and claw the cubs out of the family. The "youngsters" get the message. It almost sounds like a normal human household with teenagers!

Other animals (such as birds) abandon their young adults or kick them out of the nest. It seems the animal world has a lot to say about growing up. When it's time, it's time. No mincing words . . . just a bite, grunt, or boot to see the young off. Working their way out of a parenting job is not a debatable issue. It's interesting to note that when the young ones of any animal are gone and have assumed adult status, the parents treat them as adults. I hear many teenagers saying "amen" to that! As a matter of fact, so say many adults regarding their own parents!

Human beings can spend a lifetime leaving home. Often the biblical admonishment to "leave and cleave" never takes hold. Today there is no set time to kick the kids out of the nest or to run them up a tree. In fact, more and more young adults are living at home well into their twenties. Mom and dad find that they are still not out of a job, even after 25 years of parenting!

The Bible instructs parents to "train up a child. . . ." This implies that parents should have a plan and put it into effect. Yet as we noted earlier, there are few training grounds for parents to develop a plan in training up their children. We can just do what our parents did, and that's what seems to come most naturally for all of us. The problem is that we reflect both the positive and the negative aspects of our parents' training. We find ourselves walking in the same parental shoes they did without even realizing it. This was painfully shown in the Wayne family.

The five of them sat in tension-filled silence as I asked, "If you could change one thing in this family that would make it better for each of you, what would it be?"

After looking at each other to see who would venture out first, the oldest daughter, 19-year-old Debbie, said, "I wish Dad would quit babying me. He always has a lecture for me and never approves of anything I do. I've never once heard 'Good job.' I don't think he knows how to say it."

The two younger teenage brothers seemed to nod in agreement.

I turned to the father and said, "It seems as if the kids need your approval and acceptance."

"I've heard that before," he replied slowly. "It's hard for me to give it. I never got it when I was young."

"You didn't hear encouraging words from your parents?"

"No, not from my dad. I knew what I did wrong or what was just not good enough—he would be sure to remind me. But I never received anything positive from my father. I guess no response from him was as good as it got."

"I'll bet it still hurts when you think about it," I stated. "You know what your kids feel like when they say the same about you."

Fighting back tears he acknowledged, "I know. But it's like I don't know how to do it. I know they need to hear approval from me, but it's so hard to give."

The parenting we received plays a major role in our own parenting "blueprint," both good and bad. The old saying "You're just like your father" is so often true.

To become a parent in control, it is imperative that we have a plan. We may read instructions on putting together toys, tools, furniture, and household appliances, but when it comes to parenting—the most important job on earth—there are few practical manuals. What is your plan to work your way out of a job? As you read the rest of this chapter, you will get a handle on one blueprint to use.

## WHEN ARE YOU OUT OF A JOB?

Let's try an exercise. Get a piece of paper and a pencil. Lay the paper horizontally in front of you. Draw a line from left to right almost the entire length of the sheet. Now place a zero at the left edge of the line and leave the right end alone, similar to the line shown on the next page.

0 _____

The zero represents the birth of your baby. Welcome to parenthood! At the other end of the line write a number that indicates the age your child will be when you are finished with parenting . . . in other words, when you are out of a job.

Think about this for a minute: "What is my plan to work myself out of parenting? At what age will my children be on their own? How old will I be then?" Those are sobering questions, aren't they?

When I ask these questions in a seminar, hands rise up all over the room. "What do you mean? We are never finished!" parents protest. That's the point! Many parents are never out of a job, and that's the problem. The Bible says to "train up." It almost conveys the idea of a boot camp. Boot camp lasts only so many weeks and then the recruits are expected to move on to their responsibilities. The drill instructor is similar to the mother bear. Yet some moms and dads keep their children in boot camp, continuing to train them and never releasing the "recruits" into the regular army.

In one respect it's true that you are never through with parenting. Children will always look to their parents for some guidance and instruction. The key question to ask yourself is this: *When will I be finished with the responsibility of totally caring for my children and being completely responsible for them?*

It's like using the clutch in your car. If you release it too quickly, the car jerks forward. If you let it go too slowly, the car barely creeps ahead.

Some parents choose the age of 18 to chase their cubs (teenagers) up a tree. That's when young people graduate from high school and: (pick one) begin to work, join the Army, get married, go to college, travel the world, or live at home as if nothing has changed. The majority of parents I have polled choose 22 to 25 years of age. This is the age when most young adults graduate from college. (Of course for some there is graduate school.)

"Training up" means teaching and transferring responsibilities from the parents' shoulders to those of the children. Marguerite and Willard Beecher wrote in *Parents on the Run* that "the parents must gain their freedom from the child so that the child can gain freedom from the parents." Some children are given freedom much too early, before having learned the necessary lessons and skills to move forward successfully.

In the process of transferring responsibility from parent to child, the parent begins in total control at birth. As the parents instruct and train the child over the years, the child matures and develops self-control and self-discipline. The parents hand over greater freedom and responsibility each year, with the child becoming progressively more independent and self-sufficient. The parental task changes from a position of total control at infancy to one of influence and guidance in adulthood.

In describing the movement from control to influence, Ken Poure uses the term "progressive permissiveness." Each year on a child's birthday he diagrams a "birthday box." Whatever is put into the box is the child's total responsibility, such as taking out the trash, cleaning up the bedroom, handling money, staying out until 10 P.M., using the phone, buying clothes, and so on. The items given over to the child are contingent upon how well he has taken care of his responsibilities during the previous year. The family then has 12 months to talk about what goes into next year's "birthday box." Each year the box grows larger. This is an orderly plan for giving a child more responsibility as he grows and matures.

Fritz Ridenour in his book *What Teenagers Wish Their Parents Knew About Kids* talks about "negotiable responsibility." He says that we begin to negotiate the areas of responsibility early in a child's life. Putting away toys, brushing teeth, and setting the table are areas he calls the "child's domain of responsibility." The more capable and responsible the child becomes, the larger his domain of responsibility grows.

A key point that Fritz makes is that ideally parents continue to have the right to decide what areas are negotiable and what areas are not. This is based on the child and teenager's ability to make responsible choices based on his past behavior. If your 15-year-old daughter has been adhering to the curfew you have set for her, then she can be given more freedom and responsibility in this area. But if she has been "blowing it," then obviously nothing changes.

Let's go back to the line you drew. Place an X on the line for each year of your child's life (choose just one of your kids for this). Do some brainstorming with your spouse or another parent and write next to each yearly mark, beginning with his next birthday, a responsibility you would like to transfer to your child. Before you start, ask yourself these questions:

1. What areas is my child completely responsible for?
2. What areas am I (we) responsible for and in control of?
3. What areas might be negotiable?
4. What seems to be our biggest battleground?

It's tough to think about transferring responsibility for a child's life over to him or her. To "train up" you need a plan. A plan takes prayer, thought, energy, consistency, patience, and a goal. As you work through the rest of this chapter and the following chapters, a plan for your "de-parenting" procedure will emerge. Set your sights on your child's future independence and start enjoying his or her growing sense of mastery and competence.

## GIVING YOUR CHILD RESPONSIBILITY

A question I am often asked by parents is "How can I help my child now so he won't use drugs or alcohol when he's a teenager?" Although there is no guarantee that he won't at least experiment, the ability to make well-thought-out choices and withstand peer pressure comes through having a wholesome self-image. How you feel about yourself—how much you like or dislike yourself—has an effect on your self-image. And the choices a person makes often reflect this self-image.

Psychologist Maurice Wagner, author of *The Sensation of Being Somebody*, believes that three essential feelings lay the foundation for a strong, positive self:

1. *I belong.* I feel wanted, accepted, cared for, and enjoyed by my parents and other people.
2. *I am worthwhile.* I count, have value, and make a difference in my parents' and other people's lives.
3. *I am competent.* I can make decisions, I am adequate, and my parents and other significant people have confidence in me.

Giving your children your trust through handing over more and more responsibility is a critical factor in saying to them, "I believe you can do this; you are competent." A child who does not have the feeling he is in control has an inadequate view of himself. He has not learned to trust his ability to make choices and take control of his life. His parents did not teach him to be in control, make choices, and take risks. They did not give him the opportunities to forge out on his own, trusting him to do his best.

Margaret Mead, the great anthropologist, said that our culture is a rapidly changing one in which styles, skills, ideas, and knowledge become dated very quickly. This seems to make raising and training children virtually impossible because we do not know what specific skills and strategies to teach. "Ugh! that *New Math*!" one parent exclaimed. "I can't get past the first page in her textbook. How am I supposed to help my child when I can barely understand the table of contents?" Mead suggests that the greatest legacy we can provide our children and adolescents is to teach them how to cope and deal with change. If we cannot teach children what specific decisions they will have to make and what particular ideas they should think and learn, then perhaps we should concentrate upon teaching them "how to think," "how to learn," and "how to make decisions." Working your way out of a job means teaching your children these "how to's" and giving them the freedom to try. And remember, since no two kids are alike, *working your way out of a job is never done exactly the same way twice!*

To teach children to make their own choices you must first give them opportunities to watch *you* make choices. Young people learn first by observation and imitation. Too often children are shut out of the family decision-making process. They hear the decree but never get to see or be a part of how the final results are decided upon. Where to go for dinner on a tight budget, how to balance a checkbook, buying a car or TV set, writing checks, paying bills, and making grocery shopping lists are just a few of the many teaching opportunities available to you and your children. How are they to begin to take charge of their lives if they don't know what it takes to make good decisions and then to learn from the results of these choices?

In addition to letting them watch you make decisions, encourage them to help you. For example, if you need to go grocery shopping, your youngster can write down the items as you say them or sort the food coupons. He or she can help you find the best prices at the store and learn to be a smart shopper. It does take time and effort to let them in on the process of choosing and deciding, and it sometimes seems more work than it's worth. Yet in the process of working your way out of a job, the confidence you'll gain in their ability to make choices will pay off. Your kids may not want to take the time either, but if you can inject some fun into it, that will make these times more enjoyable for both of you.

One couple I know uses Monopoly money to teach their older children how the family money is spent. They sit down at the first of the month with the bills and a stack of play money. The expenses are "paid" by putting the bogus cash into different piles. Savings, taxes, tithing, clothes, utilities, insurance, food, and entertainment are all taken care of with the kids' participation. The kids can be heard saying things like "You mean that much goes for the house payment?" and "How come there's no money left?"

Another ingredient in teaching your children to be decision-makers is letting them learn from their mistakes. One mother of a 16-year-old girl said, "I can't stand to see her get hurt. I want to save her from all the pain I went through." On the other hand, a 15-year-old boy told his father, "I want to find things out for myself. I don't want you telling me what will happen and why. Let me do it!" In a later chapter we will talk about two of the best teaching techniques: natural and logical consequences.

The final and most important ingredient is trust. It's a fallacy that kids have to earn our trust; we *give* it to them. If your position is that kids must earn your trust, you are saying "guilty until proven innocent." The message becomes one of mistrust, not confidence. Yes, kids will mess up. So do you and I! But read 1 Corinthians 13 and you will find that love "keeps no record of wrongs . . . always protects, always trusts, always hopes, always perseveres" (verses 5,7 NIV). When we really think about it, we don't have a choice. As Fritz Ridenour has said, "You might as well trust your teenager. You don't have a reasonable alternative."

This is not to say that we wink and look the other way when kids violate house rules. Trust is not an excuse to be stupid! The focus is on *behavior*, on whether the youngster is responsible enough to stay within the bounds set by the parents and the child or teenager. "You did it again; I can't trust you anymore" can instead become "You were one hour late for a second time. This tells me you can't handle this responsibility. It looks like we have to renegotiate our contract" (or whatever consequences you have set up).

When you really analyze it, you probably trust your child more than you think you do. We tend to focus on what kids *don't* do rather than on what they actually do. Try this: Draw up a list of all the decisions that you see your child or teenager make in one day. I think you'll be amazed at how many choices he makes. After you've done this, tell him what you've done and show him your results. This would be a good time to share your confidence in him, even if some of the decisions did not work out well.

Now make a second list. This time compile all the decisions that you and your spouse make for the children or teenagers—items such as bedtime, toothpaste brand, selection of TV shows, what time to get up, when to wash the car or cut the grass, where to go to dinner, what clothes to buy, and when to do homework. How many choices are you currently making that you could begin to hand over to them?

## WHY IT'S HARD TO GIVE UP CONTROL

You are reading this book because you want to be a good parent. Giving your son or daughter more freedom to choose and thereby risking making mistakes is frightening. Failures, hurts, pain, and disappointments are inevitable, and you cannot keep these from happening.

Many parents are handicapped by self-talk. Because you want to be the best parent you can, you have the idea (self-talk) that being a parent might mean such things as:

> I am *totally* responsible for my son or daughter's behavior. Whatever he says or does is a reflection on my parenting abilities. It's my job to protect my child from suffering—from going through disappointments, mistakes, and failures. It's also my job to sacrifice for him because his needs and welfare are more important than my own. I must guide him in all he does, and it's his job to follow my directions.

If you are having trouble with one or more of your children right now, you are probably trying to implement some of these ideas in your family. What is wrong with the ideas expressed above? They are not working. They work even less as children grow older. That's why *you* are making sure your child gets to school on time, deciding which friends he can talk to, helping him to remember his lunch money, and pushing him to do his household chores. It feels like a constant power struggle because it is!

What's the key problem here? These parental ideas define you as a good or bad parent based on the child or adolescent's behavior; your identity hinges on what the child does (or doesn't do). His feelings about himself depend upon how well he fits your demands for his behavior. He too has a lot riding on how he behaves.

It's difficult not to see our children as miniature imitations of ourselves. It's almost like we get a second chance to correct all the mistakes and personal flaws of our own and make up for our lost opportunities to go to college, get married later, join the chorus, or try out for the team. When our children become mirrors of ourselves, they can do only one of two things: *Rebel* or *imitate*. Either way, they are hindered in becoming who they need to be: a separate self. It's this adult person that can withstand the pressures of peers, drugs, corporate misdealings, affair opportunities, and slowly eroding morals.

Make it a point to *enjoy* your child's decision-making ability, his or her unique style of being in the world. He or she can make choices that will constantly surprise you, and probably already do! Your ability to tolerate acceptable differences in such things as food, clothing, music, sports, friends, and choice of classes at school will ensure a continuing dialogue between you and your children. I'm not asking you to approve of all that they do, but can they talk to you about these things without you blowing your cork? Our standards must be made clear, yet kids must also have some latitude to try on new "hats," to experiment with their new emerging selves.

To have a plan implies that we have control of our children. As they grow and mature, we "negotiate responsibilities" in accord with what their present behavior dictates. We give them trust because we love them and we know that this is the soil of acceptance and healthy self-esteem.

# 4

# How Parents Get Out of Control

"Dad," the 17-year-old daughter said sweetly, "may I have the car tonight?"

"Karen, you know what happened the last time you borrowed it," Dad replied, trying to sound firm. "You came home late. We said you'd be on restriction this weekend."

"I know, I know," she responded, "but you don't understand. I had so many people to take home. It took forever! Don't you want me to help people out?"

"Yes, but . . . "

"How can they get to Bible study unless I take them?" Karen asked.

"Well . . . let me talk to your mother," Dad replied.

"Make up your mind on your own, Dad," Karen said, knowing that Mom was in the other room. Her voice was harsh now. "You always have to ask Mom. Besides, you know I'll be home on time. We settled it, didn't we?"

"I guess we did. But you'd better be in on time tonight or your mother will have a fit!" Dad answered.

"Dad, you're great! I'll be home right on the nose!"

Karen grabbed the keys and darted out the door. Her father walked into the living room and sat down next to his wife.

"What was that all about?" Mom asked.

"Karen wanted to use the car."

"What? I thought we had her on restriction. Can't you ever be firm with her?" she said, scowling.

Dad replied sheepishly, "But I *was* firm with her. For a few minutes there I had her thinking she wasn't going to get the car keys!"

At one point in their parental lives this couple had been in control. Yet as the years passed by they had gradually lost a firm sense of what they wanted from their child. As a teenager, Karen now calls the shots. Mom and Dad are left holding the bag with feelings of helplessness and resentment toward the daughter *and* with anger toward each other.

This kind of loss of control was demonstrated in my office when a husband complained, "Our sex life is not too good."

"Tell me about it," I suggested.

"Well, ever since our son was born, two years ago, it's been downhill. We hardly ever spend time together. It's like he's come between us."

"How did that happen?" I asked.

"He would cry a lot at night when he was first born. My wife would pick him up and put him in bed with us. He's been there ever since. I can usually figure when I wake up in the morning he'll be right there between us."

"That sure would kill any interest in sex. Your child has certainly come between you two, both physically and emotionally."

Children can get control of their parents and the marriage relationship in any number of ways. Sometimes they gain the upper hand right from the start; at other times they get a grip on Mom and Dad during the teenage years. How does it start? Where do parents lose control?

## HOW IT ALL BEGAN

When your first child was born, do you remember anything he could do for himself? Unless you had an unusual baby, the infant couldn't do a thing except eat, cry, wet, and spit up. (It probably seemed like it would go on forever!) You were in total control of fulfilling all the needs the child had. You decided when to change, feed, hold, and bathe him. As a good parent you responded to his needs, even though in a sense you didn't have to. Sometimes you let him cry himself to sleep or waited another 20 minutes before feeding him. Those were all *your* choices. You were in control.

When it was time to change his diapers, you knew what you wanted. You took the child, wiped his bottom, and put on a dry diaper. Your child didn't have a say in any of this: "Mom, I'd rather hold off another hour. I have an important exercise with my rattle to finish." No. There was no choice. You as the parent followed through and changed the diaper when you decided that it was necessary.

Other activities were the same way. You controlled what your baby ate, where he played, what he played with, where he went, when he bathed, and what he wore. You were, in effect, a parent in control.

The parents of the teenage daughter mentioned earlier and the parents of the two-year-old boy mentioned above had lost control. They were not successful at making their children do what they wanted them to do. Parents like these often use a variety of approaches, all of which seem appropriate but ultimately cause them to lose control. Let's briefly examine a number of ineffective methods for controlling children and teenagers. See which ones you find descriptive of your parenting style. If you are like most of us parents, you'll find more than one in your repertoire!

## Advice

"I don't want you to make the same mistakes I made when I was your age, so let me tell you . . . " It's wonderful when our children can learn from our teaching; it's a wise person who can learn from other people's mistakes. Unfortunately, most human beings have to touch the "wet paint," even when the sign is right in front of their nose! So when we say to our children, "I think you should keep your room more clean," they probably hear that as a suggestion rather than a command.

When parents give advice instead of clearly stating what they want done, kids think, "I don't really have to do it."

On the other hand, when advice is meant as helpful information, older children (and especially teenagers) feel that it means they can't think for themselves and need a parent to help them through life. Try to wait for your kids to ask what you think they ought to do. If you want to be helpful but are not asked, use opening phrases such as "Have you thought about . . . ?" or "I wonder if this would work," or, better yet, "Would you like my opinion on this?" Be prepared, though, to get a response like "Oh, brother, here we go again!" or a rolling of the eyes accompanied by a gale-force sigh.

## Requests

Courtesy is important. It recognizes that another human being has value, worth, and dignity. Parents need to model consideration for others in what they say and how they ask for things. We would like to think that our children love us and want to please us at all times. But being polite, as much as we would like to think it should, doesn't always get the job done.

How do your children respond when you ask, "Will you you please come to the dinner table?" or "If you wouldn't mind, would you pick up your toys in the living room?" Kids will often think that you are merely making a polite request and do not really want something done or stopped. Somehow, if it's said politely, it's not a serious request. If this is the case in your house, stop being polite. Statements like "Clean your room now" imply that the kids have no choice. Once the room is clean, you can then tell them that you appreciate what they have done. Later, if you're consistent, your polite requests may be heard as clear statements of what you want done and when.

## Fortune-Telling

As adults, we know all too well what lies ahead for our children. We hope to give them a picture of what life will be like and the consequences if they continue a certain behavior or attitude. To achieve this goal a common tactic is to predict the future: "If you don't start learning how to save money, you'll end up broke like your older brother" or "You'll never go to college and have a good job unless you do that homework!" While these predictions may be true, the children are not getting the direct message that they must save money or do homework. Predictions of catastrophe rarely change behavior.

## Vague Directions

It's wonderful if you have a child who knows what you want when you want it without having to be told. Most of us, though, don't have any kids like that. Yet we would like to think that they know what we want anyway. After all, don't they love us and want to do whatever they can to make us happy at all times? Because of this belief, parents often give vague directions or guidelines and assume that their kids understand. If we say, "Come home after school," some children would know what we want. Others might interpret this statement to mean that they can be home by midnight. What does "after school" mean? As kids get older they tend to use their own definitions of behavior before they use ours.

"Be nice to your little brother" is one directive often uttered. What does "be nice" mean? It depends on whose definition of "be nice" is used. To the bigger brother it might mean that he's not to give his little brother so many bruises. *If your definition is not completely clear, the kids will use their own definition.* Other examples of unclear directions are "Get up early," "Clean your room," "Don't be home too late," "Call when you get a chance," and "Be home by dark." Let's face it—millions of dollars are paid each year by grown-ups to find loopholes in the tax code. Are kids any different in finding loopholes in our rules and directions?

## Sarcasm

There is a neat little poster that says, "Attention all teenagers! Now is the time to move out of the house and make your way into the world while you still know everything!" Unfortunately, the sarcastic approach does not give a specific direction and attacks the person's character, not the problem. I often hear parents in counseling sessions use sarcastic labels such as "lazy bum," "troublemaker," and "insensitive." Parents use sarcasm out of hurt, anger, revenge, or desperation. However, instead of getting children and teenagers to do what we want, this technique breeds resentment, bitterness, and low self-esteem.

When a parent says, "Go ahead and spend the money, Mr. Know-It-All!" does the child hear that he is not to spend money? Or does a statement such as "You couldn't think your way out of a paper bag" communicate confidence that the teenager will make a good decision? Sarcasm is not effective at getting our kids to do what we want them to do. In addition, trite phrases such as "Get it together," "Lighten up," and "Shape up" are equally ineffective. What does "Get it together" mean, anyway?

When we feel out of control, we often want a scapegoat. Sarcasm seems to give us that feeling of getting back in control by blaming the child or teenager for what we cannot get him to do. But rather than regaining control, a sharp and hurtful tongue pushes young people farther away. Job cried out, "How long will you vex and torment me and break me in pieces with words?" (Job 19:2 AMP). I pray that our children are not saying the same things about us.

## Threats

You can always tell a threat by the word "if": "If you do that one more time, I'm going to tell your father when he gets home" or "If you play with that again you're going to get it." Usually threats don't work. Instead, the child ends up ignoring the statement; he sees it as a scare tactic, not as something that will be acted upon. Threats are not effective without consistent follow-through. Children learn to play the odds that nothing will happen. Imagine if the police force used only threats without much action! We wouldn't get that lump in our throat and a cold chill down our spine when we see the flashing red light in our rearview mirror!

When you say "if" you are giving the child control. Statements such as "You can have dessert *if* you finish your dinner" or "*If* you get your homework done you can watch TV" give a child the option to either do what you say or else not follow directions and take the consequences, if any. When you give a child this choice, you must be sure that you are comfortable with *either* alternative. As parents we must decide what choices we will present to our kids and what behaviors are nonnegotiable. After all, being a parent in control means controlling what options we let our children exercise. The older they become, the more options we let them have.

## Motivation

Cheerleading is fun! It's exciting to encourage another person on to greater things. It seems that if we could inspire a child enough, he would want to do what we want him to: Excitement is contagious. Yet the problem is that we cannot control children's emotions and make them *want* to forge ahead, take that risk, or go the extra mile. We can only influence and provide support. "I want my son to enjoy working in the yard," says a father. "After all, I did it when I was young. It's part of being in a family." I agree that it would be nice if Junior liked to pull weeds, clean up dog messes, and cut the grass, but I don't like doing these things myself, and I don't know anybody who gets excited when he thinks about spending a Saturday doing such chores.

I frequently have parents tell me they want their child or teenager to like school. "His attitude about school has really changed this year since he started junior high," one mother complained. "He doesn't want to work anymore and his grades have slipped quite a bit. He used to like school, but now all he wants to do is ride his skateboard." We cannot *make* our youngsters like church, youth group, certain foods, washing the car, cleaning the dishes, or making their beds. But we can require that they perform certain household chores, get a particular grade average, or go to school every day. But can't they like it and do it with a smile? Sorry! It's an axiom of psychology that when behavior changes, attitudes often follow along. Work on behavior first, and a civil attitude won't be far behind.

## Rewards

We all like to be rewarded or reinforced for what we accomplish. In fact, there is a reward or a payoff in everything we do. Jobs provide income and personal satisfaction for most people. Finishing a household project, completing a college class, or following through on a church ministry all have positive rewards or gains. Even negative behavior has a payoff. The noisiest kid in class gets something for his effort . . . attention and detention! A wife will often get angry or pick a fight with her inattentive husband just to get some interaction, or to see if he is even alive.

Rewards come in many sizes and shapes. Older children are motivated by money, a chance to go to a friend's house, TV time, or a new stereo. Smaller children like to get candy, "happy faces," play money, stickers, gold stars, points, or a trip to the ice cream store. Reinforcements work when used thoughtfully and systematically. Gold-star charts for younger children and contracts with older children and teenagers are excellent methods to organize household jobs and homework while providing for rewards. Problem behaviors such as bed-wetting, whining, teasing, and inappropriate school behavior can be set up and effectively monitored using behavioral systems and reinforcement. Charts and contracts also help to keep Mom and Dad on track in the reward system.

Unfortunately, we forget that there is often a consequence in not doing what we have asked our kids to do. For example, saying "You can watch TV tonight when you have picked up your room" gives the child a choice: Pick up his room and get TV; don't pick it up and no TV. The payoff for not cleaning the room might be that Mom will forget about it in 30 minutes and do it herself, or that the child may enjoy feeling in control and seeing Mom frustrated. She has not really told the child to pick up the room, but just to make a choice. Remember, if you give children a choice, you must be prepared to live with the choice they make!

This may sound like double-talk, but it's not. As children grow older they begin to challenge what parents want from them. When kids feel their freedom being robbed by Mom and Dad's requests, they react by dragging their feet, "forgetting," arguing, changing the subject, and becoming emotional—anything except doing what they're told. The kids' reward comes through these kinds of behavior. Your reaction to them is often the reward they seek! With problem behaviors, focus on the *behavior* you want, not on the forgetting, arguing, or changing the subject.

## Twenty Questions

If I could forbid the use of one word by parents, it would be the word "why." Questions that start off with this word invite blaming, lying, and scapegoating. The feelings it invokes are fear, guilt, and self-consciousness. "Why" questions rarely deal with the issue. "Why were you late tonight? Your curfew is midnight, and it's now 12:45. Where were you?" Do you want an answer? Okay, pick one: a) I ran out of gas, b) I didn't have a dime to call, c) I'm not in control of who's driving, d) my watch stopped, or e) I thought the curfew was changed to 1 o'clock so I would be early and you would be proud of me!

Questioning begs the issue. To be a parent in control means to deal with behavior, not excuses. Cars do break down, people do run out of gas, and so on. We need to be understanding and sympathetic. Yet *if this is a pattern* for your child, whether it's a curfew, staying after dark at a friend's house, or emptying the dishwasher, we must deal with behavior. When Jesus asks, "When I was naked, did you clothe me, or when I was hungry, did you feed me?" will He be looking for excuses? Of course not! We must likewise teach our children responsibility for their actions.

Statements such as "Why were you late tonight?" can be changed to "You were 45 minutes late tonight." "Why haven't you done your homework yet?" can be restated to "You have not done your homework." At this point you tell the child or teenager what you want in clear and concise terms. "Do your homework now" is clear; "Why didn't you do it?" invites excuses. This doesn't mean that we throw feelings out the window. A parent could respond, "I understand you forget to look at your watch. That's easy to do when you're having fun. The fact remains, though, that you are late." Don't disregard their feelings, yet don't get sidetracked off the primary issue, the behavior in question.

## WHAT WORKS

As you've read this chapter, certain phrases rang true. Yet if all of these communications prove ineffective, what works? It's simple, yet profound:

*In the important issues, your children have no choice.* When they were infants, did they choose to take a bath, pick certain clothes, and decide where to have their diapers changed? Of course not! *You* were in control. *You decided when, what, where, why, and how!*

Certain key ingredients can be seen in force with every parent who is in control. These elements form the basis for what follows in the rest of this book. Interestingly, you used each one of them when your child was an infant. First, you knew what you wanted to accomplish. *A goal was clear in your mind.* Change diapers, wear certain clothes, take a bath, lie down for a nap, eat specific foods, don't touch hot objects and sharp knives, and so on. *You were in control and knew the plan.*

At the same time, *you* decided which things were not as important. Perhaps it didn't matter what outfit to wear today, whether to feed right now, or whether to play in the kitchen or living room. It's just as important to decide what's *not* a big issue and what's *not* worth enforcing as it is to know what it is that you want to accomplish. Behaviors that you have decided not to enforce can be left to the discretion of the child or teenager. If six-year-old Jimmy has some money to spend at the store, how much say do you want to have in this decision? If a child is asked to take out the garbage, is there a specific time for it to be done, or is anytime before bedtime okay?

Second, when you were in control *you* made your intentions come true. Accomplishing what *you* want your children to do is what being in control is all about. Having a goal is the start, making it happen is the next step. Threats, advice, questions, fortune-telling, requests, sarcasm, cliches, rewards, and vague directions don't get chores done, homework finished, and rules enforced. Your infant or toddler didn't stand a chance when you really wanted him to take that bath or keep his hands off the hot stove. It was too important not to make it happen.

I continue to be amazed at the parents who drag their screaming teenager into a counseling session, then remark, "Dave, we can't get him to do a thing!"

I then ask with a slight grin, "Well, how did you get him here today?"

Looking puzzled, they reply, "We made him. We said, 'You are going to go, period.' He knew we meant business. And we followed through." This is precisely the point: They did mean business and the teenager knew it. He had no choice!

Third, you were consistent in following through with the things you wanted done. When the baby was wet you decided to change him, and then went ahead and did it. As little Junior got older, he had to take a bath each night, no questions asked. There were certain things that Junior knew were not negotiable, period.

So the key elements to your original control as a parent were that you knew what you did and did not want, you made it happen, and you were consistent.

Parents begin losing control when they don't know what behaviors they want from a child. They feel lost as to how to get the child to do specific tasks or obey set rules; the youngster now has a choice, and he often chooses not to do what Mom and Dad want. These parents don't follow through and see that a chore, curfew, or task gets accomplished, no matter what. To make matters worse, they are not consistent in enforcing these rules from day to day.

So how do we gain control? In the next chapter we'll tackle the first key ingredient: choosing the specific behaviors you want and must have from your children.

# 5

# If You Don't Know
# Where You're Going

As I sat in a restaurant with my wife and two children, a couple with three small children came in and sat next to us. We began talking with the parents, and during the course of the conversation one of them asked, "Are you two planning to have any more children?"

Jokingly I replied, "I don't think so. My psychiatrist says it's hazardous to my health!"

With a deep sigh the father responded, "Well, if you decide to have another, don't. It's so much more crazy with three than with two. In fact, three children is the best reason for not having fun!"

It's almost amusing that as a psychologist and family therapist I frequently hear statements from parents with one child wishing they had two, or those with two children thinking that three would be wonderful. Yet no matter how many children you have or wish you didn't have, you can still feel out of control!

Parenting is at least an 18-year job. The goal is the transfer of responsibility from the parents' shoulders to the child's. As kids grow and mature, they take on more freedom and more decision-making ability. Parents are less and less in the picture; they move from a relationship of complete control during their child's infancy to one of advisory influence as the child reaches adulthood.

Right now you are at a point where some of your child's behaviors are a problem. And it's your job as a parent to decide what to do about it. Unfortunately, many parents default and let the child decide whether to clean up the bedroom, get up on time for school, feed the dog, or set the dinner table.

*You need to decide who is going to decide.*

This is a key ingredient in regaining control! Once you've figured out what behaviors you must have, the other things that the child does become his or her responsibility.

## WHAT DO YOU WANT FROM YOUR CHILD?

Make a list of things your child does that bother you. If you have more than one youngster, then make a list for each child. If there are two parents, then make two separate lists, since what bothers one parent may not be a problem to the other. There will be a lot of overlap between the two lists, yet a few distinct items will show up. What you do with these lists will form the foundation for you to regain control. To get your creative juices going, I have listed a number of behaviors that parents have reported as problems in their households:

Makes rude noises at dinner
Won't brush his teeth
Screams and yells at bedtime
Won't do his homework
Fights with her brother
Has a bad attitude
Has to be reminded to do chores
Doesn't feed the dog
Won't clean up her room
Will not hang up his clothes
Leaves wet towels in the bathroom
Watches too much TV
Leaves my tools outside
Calls me names
Sneaks out at night
Leaves his toys outside
Won't make her bed
Doesn't take a bath
Takes money out of my wallet
Won't do things with the family
Has temper tantrums
Tells lies
Wears my clothes without asking
Won't put dishes in the dishwasher

Stays at home all the time
Doesn't have any friends
Interrupts people when they are
    talking
Plays the stereo too loud
Will not come home right after school

In helping parents decide what behaviors they want changed, I always ask them to describe the things their children are doing that bother them. The list you have made is such an exercise. As parents tell me about problem areas, they often use a variety of vague terms such as lazy, angry, rebellious, defiant, problem child, withdrawn, bad attitude, low self-esteem, poor self-image, moody, slow learner, or clown. The difficulty with these terms is that while I know what they mean to me, I don't know what they mean to other moms and dads. What characterizes a lazy child to one parent could be a hard-working child to another. An angry child to one adult might be described by another parent as intense and feisty.

John, age 12, was brought to my office for counseling by his mother and father. When I asked about the problem, they described him as having a "bad attitude."

"What does he do that makes you believe he's got a bad attitude?" I asked.

Mom answered, "He doesn't seem to like anything. He doesn't like school anymore, or our home, or us."

"What *exactly* is he doing that's been bothering you lately? Describe to me some examples of what you are talking about; give me a word picture."

"Well, he doesn't like to do his homework or his household chores."

"Do you want him to like these things?" I asked.

"Of course we do," she replied, seeming puzzled by the question.

"Getting him to do something is one thing, but making him like it is quite another."

"Okay," she said, "he *will not do* his homework. When he does, he puts if off to the last minute. And I never know if he has any work to do or not."

At this point the parents began to realize that *behaviors* were what I needed to hear about, not attitudes. None of us could make John like homework or want to be with the family. That would be a frustrating and futile battle. But I could help them change John's behavior. By clarifying the behaviors which were of concern to them, the parents were then able to establish clear goals for their son. Remember:

*Focus on specific behavior, not on attitudes!*

Review your list and note behaviors that are vague and general. Rewrite these items so they're specific. For example, if you wrote, "He doesn't clean up his room," you might rewrite it to say, "He doesn't make the bed or put the dirty clothes in the hamper, and leaves food in his room." Now you have identified three specific behaviors to work on. If you wrote, "She fights with her brother," make it more specific: "She kicks her brother under the dinner table and goes into his room without asking his permission."

Now comes the hard part: deciding which behaviors you must insist upon and which behaviors you will let the child choose for himself. It's impossible to change all the troublesome items at once, so you must decide which behaviors are most important. Examine your list and rank the problem areas, beginning with number one (the most important). What often happens is that when parents learn to control their children in the top one, two, or three behaviors, the kids realize that Mom and Dad mean what they say, and then change comes more easily on the rest of the items. In addition, it's more effective if you address one behavior at a time. You'll get overwhelmed if you tackle a handful of problems all at once.

How do you decide which behaviors to choose? First, make sure that the ones you choose to work on are carried out. Once you have chosen number one, *you cannot stop until you get what you want.* You must do whatever it takes to change the behavior! Therefore it is essential that you select behaviors with great care. You want your child to realize, "My folks mean business, and they aren't going to give up on this one."

Second, ask yourself, "Do I have any direct power over the situation?" Problems you have direct control over might include TV-watching, raiding the refrigerator, putting toys away, brushing teeth, leaving dirty dishes in the living room, and coming to the breakfast table on time. If your teenager smokes cigarettes while out of the house, there's no direct action you can take to change that. You can forbid him or her from smoking in the house, in the garage, or on the premises. If you discover that he has been smoking you can cut his allowance, make him wash his own smelly clothes, ground him, or even search his room for cigarettes. It all depends on how far you want to go in changing his behavior. You may not have total control, but that does not mean you have no control!

If your daughter continues to borrow your clothes after you have asked her not to, you do have some direct power over the situation. In seminars I've conducted, parents have suggested a variety of effective tactics to combat this problem: Stop lending her the clothes, make her pay for the cleaning bill out of her allowance, put a lock on your door, or make her change every time you see her in your clothes.

Third, when you can let go and live with a particular situation, give the child a choice. You must ask yourself, "At what age will I let my son be responsible for his bedroom . . . or his bike, skateboard, car insurance, homework, church attendance, bedtime, debts, and promptness to class?" Kids are often a good barometer of when to let go and what to let go of. In listening to their requests (or gripes) for things like more time to play outside, later bedtimes, more allowance money, or greater freedom or privacy you can hear areas of responsibility to begin giving them.

A counselor friend of mine has said that *parents must pick their battles wisely or they'll be battling all the time*. Over what do you find yourself continually battling? If being five minutes late on curfew is worth the fight, then enforce it. If the lateness is perpetual, and it's important to you, then of course it's worth enforcing. But if the young person is typically on time, then it's a judgment call. *Let their behavior dictate what freedoms you allow.*

When you give your youngster greater responsibility, he has the option to do what you would like him to do or not do. We see this principle with God Himself, who has given us the ability to make choices. We don't always do what He wants us to do, yet He allows us this freedom. In the same way, optional rules give freedom to our child. They play a greater and greater role as the child matures and grows into adulthood. Suggestions such as "I'd like you to do more homework" leave the choice up to the individual; they sound like an option. "I wish you would give the dog a bath" gives the child a choice to do it or not to do it—another option. Can you live with your child's choices? You need to live with them more and more as he or she grows older. That's what growing up and letting go is all about!

Behaviors that we *must* have from our kids are not options. Yet the "option" category of behaviors can be an effective method of discipline. The option gives the child a choice: "If you do this, then that will happen." This method of discipline includes logical consequences, natural consequences, spanking, rewards, and reinforcement. These can all be very effective and appropriate when used thoughtfully. These methods will be discussed later in the book.

Fourth, and most important, the values we choose as Christian parents are reflected in the behaviors we want from our children. Proverbs 22:6 tells us to "train up" our children. The idea is that parents are to have a plan.

In Philippians chapter 4 the apostle Paul exhorts believers to dwell on truth, purity, right behavior, excellence, and honor. These values are modeled to our children by us. We become the first living examples to them of what God is like. One of the clearest examples of parenting values was taught by Jesus in the parable of the Prodigal Son (Luke 15:11-24). Here we see God depicted as having a love that let the younger son go when he asked for his inheritance. The father loved the son too much to hold him back. He knew that his love could not possess his son without imprisoning him. Our love as parents needs to be the same—a love that trusts enough to release control and at the same time demonstrates unmerited favor.

## ESTABLISHING YOUR RULES

The few items you've selected and ranked now become rules. A good rule protects and teaches a child at the same time. The youngster who is told not to pull the dog's tail is protected from a nasty nip or bite while being taught the animal's need not to be treated like a rag doll.

Children need to know your rules; *you* need to know your rules. God gave the children of Israel His rules on stone tablets. I'm not suggesting that you put yours on tablets of stone. After all, they wouldn't hang too well on the refrigerator door! Yet they must be clear and must deal with *behavior*. A statement such as "I want you to like school" is a want or a wish, not an enforceable rule. "Please be polite to your sister" is getting closer, yet who knows what "polite" means? The child's understanding of "polite" is often not the same as the parents'. When you break down "polite" into specific behaviors, then you can be more precise. For example:

"Do not ever enter your sister's room without her permission. If you need to get something, then come and ask me first." If your rule is not clear, then your kids will use their own definition of what the rule means.

Your rule must deal exclusively with behavior and must tell the child what to do or not do. Notice that you are not including any rewards, punishments, logical consequences, or natural consequences. The rules you choose as your *must rules* provide no choice for the child. Other forms of discipline leave a choice; they give the child an option. If you want the child to have a choice, then use one of the other methods.

Write a rule below using the item you ranked number one from your list:

*Rule number one is:*


Now try to think like your child. If you were to ask her to state this rule in her own words, what would she say? Chances are that she would state it to her own advantage, leaving out important parts of the rule. What parts? Things like when, how often, where, how, how well, how much, with whom, and so on. *These are key ingredients in any rule.*

For example, if the rule you wrote above said, "Come home after school," how would your child interpret it? If what you had in mind was for her to be home by 3 P.M., then say so. A rule such as "Clean your room every day" leaves the child a lot of freedom. How well must he clean it? Should he clean it before or after school? Is as late as 10 P.M. okay?

I've listed below some statements that parents use to try to get their children and teenagers to do what they want them to do. Read them over and see how you might restate the rules so there is no question in anyone's mind about what they mean. At the end of the chapter you'll find these rules rewritten to be more specific and to close the loopholes.

1. If you leave those dishes in your room again, you'll miss dinner next time.
2. I'd like some help cleaning the garage today.
3. Call me when you get a chance.
4. You're late again.
5. Your room looks awful!
6. If I were you, I'd do some homework.

Now go back to your rule and rewrite it below, adding any key elements that apply, such as what to do, when to do it, how well to do it, where to do it, and how often it is to be done.

*Rule number one is:*


Suppose your rule concerns cleaning the table after dinner. Your child's idea of a clean dinner table is probably not your idea of a clean table. This means that you must show him step-by-step. Yes, he has seen you do it millions of times and should know how to do it, but does he? Be as specific as possible, showing him exactly what he is to do. A rule on cleaning off the dinner table might say:

"Each night after dinner, Monday through Friday, you are to clear the dinner table of any dishes, silverware, napkins, drinks, cups, and food, so that the table is completely free of anything left over from dinner. Then you are to wipe the tabletop so it is clean and shiny, with no food or liquid left on it. Begin to clean the table as soon as the last person has left."

Now comes a critical point. Ask your child to tell you what it is that you want done. *Checking his perception of the rule is very important!* You will save yourself a lot of headaches when you double-check the rule. In addition, when it's time to discipline, you will have more conviction about carrying through because you know that he knew exactly what was required. When in doubt, check it out!

You might need to recite this rule daily for two weeks or more. Eventually your child will get the message that you mean business. After a while you can say, "Clean the table off now." In a few more weeks you will be able to say, "Please clean the table now." Eventually you won't have to say anything; the child will comply with the rule on his own.

If you want the table cleaned, and this is a *must behavior*, then the child has no choice. But if you want the child to like cleaning the table and maybe even whistle while he is doing it, then I've got some swampland in Florida to sell you. Remember, the focus is on *behavior*, not attitudes. The positive feelings that result from responsible behavior will eventually come, but don't lose any sleep watching for them!

Another important point is that the rule must match the age-level capabilities of the child. A five-year-old cannot clean his room as effectively as a ten-year-old. Yet he can put his toys away and place his dirty clothes in a hamper. One way to find out what he is capable of doing is to ask him to do it. If it seems that he is doing his best and sticking to the task without getting discouraged, then he can abide by the rule. Another way to find out what is age-appropriate is to ask other parents what they expect from their children. You might also ask his schoolteachers to help you in choosing certain tasks. Watching your child and others in his class is a great way to get good ideas about what kids are able to do and how well they can do it.

Now try writing a second rule. This time be sure to include action words like quit, stop, now, never, always, take, go, do, make, etc. The fewer words you use the better, yet the first time you state the rule may require more explanation for younger children. Remember to include, if appropriate:

- what
- when
- where
- how
- how often
- how much
- how long
- how well

*Rule number two is:*

Now look over the rule. Is it mandatory or optional? Are you willing to enforce it or not? Does it have direction and action to it? Is the child capable of doing it?

And . . . this is the acid test . . . what is your child or teenager's definition of the rule? How has he interpreted what you want?

I mentioned that Ken Poure developed what he called a "birthday box." Whatever is in the box is the child's responsibility; whatever is outside the box is the parents' responsibility to enforce. It's important to enlarge the box as children get older. Your rules need to be reviewed by the family members periodically—on birthdays, new school years, first of the summer, every quarter, or even weekly. Your children's performance during the past year, quarter, or week will dictate whether you should give them greater freedoms. Provide your children and teenagers with the opportunity to periodically talk to you about the rules and regulations in the household. If there are many jobs to do, you might allow them to pick, swap, take on, or give up certain tasks.

Now that you have written your second rule, go ahead and write three more. When you are ready, sit down with your children and explain the first rule. Don't give them any more rules at this time. Work on only one at a time. You might introduce it by saying, "I've noticed I have been on your backs a lot lately about cleaning your rooms. I don't like yelling at you and I know you don't like hearing me! What I'm going to do is decide with each of you when you will clean your room, how well and how often. For instance, Tim, every Saturday morning by 9 A.M. you are to vacuum your floor so I can see all the carpet, take all your dirty laundry to the laundry room and put it in the hamper, and dust your furniture with a clean rag and polish so I can see a shine on it. It's not fair of me to expect you to clean your room anytime *I* want you to. You need to know in advance when to have it done and how well."

When you have presented your first rule to each child, *have him restate the rule*. What is his perception of this rule? He may put it in his own words, but that's not good enough. You want it in your words! In addition, you may have to walk him through the task step-by-step to be sure he knows what you want. Your idea of clean and his idea may not be the same. To expect him to automatically do the job the way you want it done is not realistic. So take the time to show him.

You'll notice that I mentioned working out the rule with *each* child. Letting the child help make the rule is a good idea. Children can often tell you when they would like to clean the room, do homework, talk on the phone, or feed the dog. The more input you allow the kids, the greater the chance that you will not have to enforce a particular rule. In doing this you're saying, "I realize that you too have needs and are busy. I'm willing to understand and recognize what you want. Let's put our heads together and come up with a plan."

In a later chapter we will look at turning over to your child or teenager some of the bothersome items you wrote on your list. This is where the other methods of discipline come into play, such as logical consequences. Certain behaviors need to enter into the youngster's domain of responsibility as you work your way out of a job.

In Chapter 6 we will look at follow-through on *must behaviors*. In demanding that a child do what you want him to do, you must be willing to follow through to insure that the job is finished. Some parents are great at stating clear directions, yet that is not enough, as we shall see.

Now here are the statements from earlier in this chapter that I've rewritten to be more precise. In some cases consequences could be added, but they are not added here. The focus is on constructing clear and concise rules.

1. Pick up the dirty dishes in your bedroom and put them in the dishwasher now. Never leave dishes in your room.
2. By 5 o'clock this afternoon, I want you to sweep the garage floor using a broom and dustpan. Put the dirt in the large green trash can.
3. Call me in two hours, which will be 5 o'clock.
4. Your curfew is midnight. You are 30 minutes late. You are to be home by midnight on Friday and Saturday and by 9 P.M. Monday through Thursday.
5. Clean your room on Saturday mornings by 11 o'clock. That means bed made, floor vacuumed, and dirty clothes picked up and put into the hamper.
6. Your homework time is from 7:30 to 9 P.M. Turn the TV off now and do your homework in your room without the radio on.

# 6

# Following Through

The young mother had had enough. Her two-year-old was impossible to handle in the grocery store. After each trip it looked as if King Kong had ransacked the shelves. Everything along the aisles became fair game for those little hands. Suddenly, Mother recognized the obvious—keep the shopping cart centered down each aisle. That way her youngster's reach was too short to grab anything his heart desired. She tried it and it worked. Upon seeing the child red-faced and frustrated, arms flailing wildly, another hassled mommy remarked, "Finally, successful *arms control!*"

Often what we want and what we get from our children are two different things. In the previous chapter we began to look at what *you* want from each of your children. From a list of bothersome behaviors, you ranked several in order of importance. Number one was the behavior you would most like changed. Other items further down the list might become ones you would release and give your child the responsibility for fulfilling. That is, he would become the decision-maker for that particular area. But with those essential behaviors you want from your child, the question still hits you between the eyes: "How do I make him do it? How do I follow through?"

The parents in an earlier chapter who watched as their teenage daughter walked out to the car against their wishes were ineffective at following through on what they wanted. The young girl knew it and counted on that fact. Kids know how far they can push. If a young child asks Mommy for some candy and she says no, you can bet that Daddy will get asked next! Often he will say, "Sure, go ahead." The child gets the candy and learns an effective lesson: Mom and Dad can be pitted against each other; the system can be manipulated, and I can win.

One mother told me that her young child would usually ask for something about six times, getting progressively louder each time. "The sixth time is when I give up," she sighed. "It's too much hassle to keep saying no. I know I shouldn't give in, but I do." The score: child 1, mom 0.

Children learn early in life to manipulate. They want the freedom to have what they want and do as they please. When they find out what works to get their way, they'll use it time and time again. Bill Cosby once said,

"Give me 100 two-year-olds and I'll conquer the world!" By that age they have learned all the tricks of manipulation. Why? Because they are mean and rotten? No, because they are human beings who are self-willed and want their way. That's why the word "no" is one of the most powerful tools you have in parenting. It's the one word that teaches children that life is not just for them; there are other people on the planet as well. It moves youngsters from a self-centered view of life to an other-centered view. Jesus constantly stressed an awareness of people's needs through His talk and His action. Saying no, then, is the beginning of understanding that there is a "me" and there is a "you."

## HOW PARENTS INVITE MANIPULATION

Parent's unwittingly create the climate for manipulation by children and teenagers. What follows are several of the most common ways that parents invite youngsters to take advantage of them.

### Passive Anger

The family was quiet as I asked the mother, "What do you do when your son doesn't do what you have asked?" Glancing over at her 14-year-old son, she replied, "I get angry and hurt."

"What does Mom do when she gets angry and hurt?" I asked the son.

"She says stuff like 'Fine, just see if I'm driving you anywhere again!' She acts like a hurt puppy and won't talk to anyone."

"What do *you* do when Mom acts this way?"

"I ignore her and do what I want. It bugs me when she puts that guilt trip on me. I just want to get away."

This mother was expressing her anger in what is called a "passive-aggressive" way. It's a subtle form of punishment. We don't say we are angry, we just get back at the perpetrator in some quiet, manipulative way. Common expressions of this style of anger are withdrawal, silence, forgetting, lateness, overeating, spending money, or staying late at work. These are all attempts to punish the other person for not doing what we wanted him or her to do. But this tactic actually invites manipulation right back. Instead of following through on what we want from our children, we exhibit passive-aggressive anger and teach them to do the same. Children may express this by forgetfulness in doing chores, lateness, sloppy work, silence, or behind-our-backs criticism.

How do you get angry? Do you withdraw your presence from someone? Do you stop talking and give him the silent treatment? Are you often late for a certain person about whom you have mixed feelings? How about your eating patterns? Do you find yourself eating when you are not hungry but have had a blowup with someone that day? Do you notice yourself forgetting to do certain things for the same people? Any of these behaviors might indicate that you are harboring some anger and resentment in a passive-aggressive manner. What you get in return won't make things any better! In fact, you probably learned these patterns from your parents, and your children will in turn learn them from you.

## It's Just a Phase

It's true that children grow through developmental stages. Swiss psychologist Jean Piaget has explored how their thinking style changes dramatically over the years. For example, the child from zero to two years has no concept of "object permanence." When an object he is observing (such as a ball) is hidden from view with a towel, he fails to look for it. To him it no longer exists. The two- to seven-year-old child begins to use symbols to represent things in his environment. The development of language is the major activity of this period of life. But limitations still exist. When he is shown two different shapes made out of the same amounts of clay, one looks larger than the other. You cannot convince him otherwise.

We hear about "the terrible two's" and "the terrific three's," or "Look out, he's almost a teenager!" While there is some validity to these stages, parents often use the "he's-just-in-a-phase" rationale as wishful thinking. They figure they can wait the stage out and hope he'll grow out of the annoying behaviors. Some kids do; others don't. The tendency is not to demand that the child stop or start doing a specific behavior, but to let the problem work itself out. But instead it often gets even more out of hand.

Six-year-old Bryan would walk by his three-year-old sister and knock her over with an elbow to the side. Bryan's parents politely asked him to "be kind" to his sister. That didn't work. Then they tried to talk to him about her feelings, wanting him to understand how his sister is affected by his behavior. That didn't work either. In desperation they offered him a reward for each day he would go without knocking her down. Unfortunately, knocking her down and hearing her "squawk" was its own reward. When I talked to the parents about this behavior, they thought it might be a stage he would grow out of.

"How long are you willing to wait for him to outgrow it?" I asked. That question caught them by surprise. I then began to show them how they had been very successful in getting Bryan to do many things that he didn't want to do by simply insisting that he do them. But he had never been told, "Stop knocking down your sister *now*."

Believe it or not, you *will* get your children to obey you by insisting upon it. Think about it for a minute. There are a number of behaviors that your son or daughter is doing because you mean business. Taking a shower, getting up for school, going to the dentist, calling from a friend's house, and attending church are just a few examples.

It's true that children develop through stages. Yet this is no excuse for behaviors that are disruptive and harmful. Ask yourself two questions: 1) How long am I willing to wait for my child to outgrow this behavior; and 2) is there good evidence that my child cannot perform the behavior based on his or her age and stage of development?

## All Children Do It

Children are often like mimes; they mimic the behavior of others. They learn through modeling what they see. It's easy for parents to say, "All children do this, so it's not so wrong." They believe that the behavior, no matter how irritating, is natural and that there is little they can do to cause the child to alter his actions. In effect, they're saying that the youngster is incapable of controlling his behavior.

One couple talked to me about how their seven-year-old girl "tattled" all the time. She had something to tell about everyone. The parents, although tired of hearing every little detail of "who did what to whom," felt that this was natural and that all kids "tattled." I asked them to offer evidence to support this belief.

"Well, I'm sure I did the same thing when I was little," the mom said in reply.

I responded by saying that all children have a need to talk about their feelings of injustice. But there is certainly no evidence to indicate that she must come running to the parents after every little infraction.

We then went on to discuss why they felt their child "tattled so much." Apparently the parents had a difficult time listening to their daughter even when she was not tattling because she talked incessantly. I advised the parents to set aside specific times to spend with her, talking about anything she wanted to. They determined that bedtime could be set aside for this purpose. Dad also made a commitment to call home once a day to see how the family was doing. In addition, *the child was told to stop tattling*. Instead, the parents would repond to her tattling by saying, "We can talk about this during our special time tonight" or "It sounds like you have a problem. What are you going to do about it?"

If you excuse your child's behavior on the grounds that all children do it, what's your evidence? Is it really true that all children do it, or do you just want to believe this?

## He's Had a Rough Childhood

By age ten Brett had endured a lot of tough times. His parents divorced when he was five, and then his mom remarried, only to divorce again when Brett was eight. He rarely saw his real father, who had also married again. His mother, Marilyn, was working full-time and receiving little financial support. The family economic picture was bleak indeed. As an only child, Brett had to weather all these family crises alone.

Marilyn came to see me because of her son's angry outbursts at home and school and his refusal to obey her. In other words, she felt out of control.

"When did Brett's behavior problems begin?" I asked.

"About the time I divorced the second time," she replied. "Brett was getting close to my second husband, and then he up and leaves. I think it wiped Brett out."

"Do you think his refusal to obey you is because of the lack of a consistent father figure in his life?"

"Yes, I do," she replied. "I think his behavior is more for attention than anything."

"Do you think you allow him to get away with misbehavior because of his stressful background?" I inquired.

"I think I sometimes do. I guess I feel so bad for him and want to make it up. It's like it's really my fault. He didn't ask for all this."

"Is allowing him to get away with more than he should helping to make up for his painful past?"

"I don't think so. He's just getting worse, and I think I compound the problem. I just feel so bad for him, and it's hard to say no," Marilyn added quietly.

"I'm sure Brett has been affected by the problems in the family, and I would like to work with him on those," I replied. "At the same time, you need to be firm with him and expect him to behave like other children. Demanding appropriate behavior is your first step."

Parents often act out of guilt and painful feelings for their children. To make up for past problems, children are allowed too much freedom to do whatever they want to do. Wanting to be tolerant, flexible, and thoughtful, parents often let their kids "get away with murder." This not only prevents them from learning appropriate behaviors, but pushes them into more troublesome misbehaviors that snowball as the child gets older. The problems don't get better, but worse.

Do you let your children get away with certain behaviors because you're trying to be sensitive to them and want to help make up for deprivations they've experienced in their childhood? You need to help them work through their thoughts and feelings about what has happened to them, while at the same time requiring appropriate behaviors.

## CHILDREN'S MANIPULATIONS

All children seem to learn the same methods of frustrating their parents' wishes. Children spend years learning to manipulate parents to get their way, and parents let them become experts at it. When a child finds out what works, you can bet he'll do it again and again. The following are some of the most common methods that children use to manipulate parents, along with steps you can take to counteract these tactics.

## Mom Versus Dad

This method is simple: Divide and conquer. When one parent says no, ask the other. But make sure the other parent doesn't know that he or she is second choice! It begins when they are small. A two-year-old asks, "Candy, Mommy?"

"No candy, Peter. We are eating dinner soon."

Little Peter finds Dad like a heat-seeking missile. The timing is right—Dad is engrossed in his newspaper.

"Candy, Daddy?"

"I don't think so."

"Candy, Daddy!"

"Go see Mommy."

"Candy, Daddy!!" Little Peter is now applying the pressure like a used car salesman.

"Okay, Peter. Susan?" he calls to his wife. "Where's the M and M's?"

You can anticipate the rest. Susan responds with a definite "No!" Dad questions her logic. Little Peter begins to cry and have a minor heart attack on the living room floor. Dad then tells Mom she's rigid and uptight. Mom gets her dander up and says Dad is nonresponsive and never supportive. The fight has begun!

When a child can pit "bad guy" Mom against "good guy" Dad, he is taking advantage of an already-present problem: the parents' lack of cooperation and together-ness. The child capitalizes on conflict in the marriage.

When Mom and Dad have two different standards of behavior for the same rule, the child has the option of choosing which standard he wants to obey. In effect, there is no rule! Mom may be trying to protect the children from Dad's temper, or Dad may be trying to protect the kids from Mom's "pickiness." In reality, the parents are expressing their anger and resentment at each other through the children. Anytime Mom and Dad are in conflict over a rule or behavior, the child "wins" and Mom and Dad are at each other's throats.

Look again at rule number one that you wrote out earlier. Do you and your spouse have the same defini-tion of this rule? Do you both want the same behavior from your child? As long as you define the rules in terms of *behavior*, not attitudes or intentions, it will be much easier to stand together and enforce the rules.

When you have both agreed on the first rule, decide how you will support each other when "attacked" by the gremlins. Get your story straight. For example, if the rule says "No candy or snacks one hour or less before dinner," both parents must know that the other will enforce the rule by saying no.

Parents don't always agree on the behaviors they want. That's when it's time to compromise. If Mom wants the dinner table cleared by the kids each night, and Dad feels that seven days a week is too much at their age, then perhaps four nights a week, Monday through Thursday, might work. Dad might feel that the children's room should be cleaned each morning: beds made, clothes picked up, desk cleaned off, shoes put away, the hamster cage cleaned, and so on. Mom might only be concerned with having the bed made and dirty clothes in the hamper each day; the other jobs could be completed on Saturday mornings. A compromise solution *must* be worked out. If it is not, any rule is doomed to failure because of one parent's passive resistance to the other's unwillingness to compromise or help out.

What if you can't come to a mutually satisfactory compromise? You essentially have three choices: 1) Let go and support the other parent's decision; 2) eliminate the rule and give the child the option of doing it on his own; or 3) seek counsel from your youth pastor, senior pastor, or marriage and family counselor.

## Arguing

Children will always challenge parental authority; that's part of growing up and breaking away from Mom and Dad. As they grow, youngsters need the opportunity to hear Mom and Dad's logic and reasons for the decisions they have made. Yet most arguments are not discussions or negotiations; they are a clash of wills: what "I want" versus what "you want."

Once we decide on what we must have and our reasons have been stated, and the other party has been heard and understood, there is no reason to argue. Kids argue for several reasons. One is to wear the parent out and get what they want. Like the pigeon pecking the handle for a kernel of grain, children will repeatedly argue when they feel they can get what they want. If this strategy gets reinforced once, it will be tried again. Parents throw their hands up and say, "Okay, if that's what you want, then go right ahead. See if I care!" The score: parent 0, child 1.

Another reason kids argue is to sidetrack the issue. "Amy, would you take the trash out tonight?" the mom asked of her ten-year-old daughter.

"How come I have to? You never make Tommy do anything! He never takes out the trash!"

"Tommy did take out the trash last night. He has his jobs to do."

"I have more to do than he does. You're not fair. You like him more than me."

What started out as a simple job request got side-tracked into who loves whom the most! This is a very common tactic in parenting and in marriages. The argument shifts from a behavior wanted to personal accusations and hurts.

A third reason for arguing is to buy time. Arguing over doing homework can put off doing the home-work. A child would rather argue with Mom or Dad, delay the task, and take a chance at getting the parents so frustrated that they give up, get sidetracked, or wear out. In this way the child gets out of doing the job.

So what should you do? First of all, realize that argu-ments are really about power. If you don't want to argue, yet find yourself arguing, who is in control? As soon as you defend yourself in an argument, then the other person has the right to defend himself and argue in return. Each person wants to defend himself and convince the other that he is wrong.

After one of my seminars, a mother took my advice. On the way home one night from church, she told her eight-year-old daughter, "As soon as we get home, you are to go directly to the bathroom and take a shower." The daughter began the usual verbal battle, yet with one difference: The "enemy" was not fighting back! The mother later told me, "I did not argue. She knew what I wanted. I usually argue with her and try to convince her she needs a shower. Convincing her was not what I wanted; her showering was!"

The best advice I can give you is: *Don't argue*. It's important that children know you understand what they are saying, yet *the behavior you want* is the goal, not their feeling understood. Greg Bodenhammer has suggested using the words "regardless" and "nevertheless" to focus on the behavior rather than the argument. He calls these words "argument deflectors." When you clearly state what you want and when you want it, use one of these words to deflect their argument back onto the desired behavior.

"Jimmy, turn off the TV now and go to your room and do your homework."

"But, Mom, I have plenty of time to do my homework. Besides, the show isn't over yet."

"I understand you enjoy this show. Watching it is certainly more fun than doing homework. Nevertheless, you know the homework rule we set up (this assumes that Mom was clear with Jimmy when the rule was set up). Turn the TV off now."

"Just wait 15 minutes. I'll go then."

"Nevertheless, turn the TV off now."

If the child won't obey, the parent goes to the TV, turns it off, and escorts the child to his room.

Other deflectors you can use are "at any rate," "the point is," "the issue is," and "yes, but." Once you have used the words with your clear direction, follow through and see that the children do as they are told. If you are stating a rule for future behavior, then state it, use a deflector, and walk away.

Practice using the deflector words. Say them as you are driving down the street or are in the shower; mumble them under your breath when your child is arguing with you.

**Forgetting**

If there is one phrase used by more children than any other, it is "I forgot." When the child looks at you with those big sad eyes and softly utters this famous statement, it's difficult to get angry at him. But if he is saying, "Well, excuse me! I forgot, Your Highness," it's much easier to blow your cork.

Forgetting is simply a way of saying, "I don't want to do it" or "It's more important to you than it is to me." The task is usually more of a priority to you, the parent, than it is to the child. After all, wouldn't you rather talk to a friend than do homework, or play with the dog than take out the trash? The fact is that forgetting is a common delay tactic designed to get Mom and Dad to either do the job themselves or give up and forget about it.

If the behavior you want is a *must*, then *you* must do whatever it takes to see that your child does the behavior. This includes staying on top of the situation so that you can see that the behavior or task is completed. "Take the trash out now" is a direct statement. Are you willing to stand there until the child does it, and even escort him out to the garbage can? Or will you argue until your voice is hoarse, then throw up your hands in disgust and let the trash build up to the height of the Sears building in Chicago? The key remains that *this* behavior is one you want; *the child does not have a choice*.

## White Lies, Black Lies, and Multicolored Lies

Lies are manipulations that children, teenagers, and even adults use to hide their behavior. Parents often get caught in the trap of trying to play detective and find out if the child is lying, instead of focusing first on the behavior in question. It becomes an exercise in diversion tactics.

One evening Mom gets a phone call from her neighbor telling her that while she was at work her son Jed had several friends visiting in the house. The rule is: No friends visiting in the house until Mom comes home at 5:30. Mom approaches Jed and says, "Jed, who were you with today after school?"

"I went over to John's house for a while. Why?"

"Is that all you did?"

"Yeah. We were over there all afternoon. Then I came home."

"You didn't do anything else?" Mom asks again.

"Here you go again. You always ask me questions like I was on trial. I hate it when you do this. You never trust me. You never believe anything I say!" Jed shouts.

"Don't start shouting at me, young man! You're lying to me. I know you were here in this house with some of your friends. You know the rule about friends in the house after school."

"I don't believe it. You love to set me up, don't you? You're so unfair!"

At this point the two are off and running in a full-blown fight. The original issue gets lost in the high decibels.

What happened in this instance was that Mom gave Jed the opportunity to lie. He was right, it *was* a setup. The point is that Jed's *behavior* is what must be dealt with first. The mother needs to present the facts and give the boy an opportunity to agree or refute the evidence. Here's how she could handle it.

"Jed, I received a phone call today. The person I talked with said you were in the house about 4 o'clock with two of your friends. You know the rule we have set up about no friends in the house until I get home."

Jed might answer, "I can't believe it! Who called you? The neighborhood FBI?"

"Who gave me the information is not the point. You are not to be in the house with friends until I get home."

"You'd believe some old crank? I wasn't here with my friends anyway. What's the use—you never listen to me!" he screams.

"Jed, I will do whatever it takes to enforce this rule," Mom firmly states. "You will not have friends in the house until I get home!"

This mom did not get diverted to any other issues; the *behavior* was the focus, not the lie. When we concentrate on the behavior, the kids will not be able to take advantage of other tactics designed to get us off track.

What if you really don't know the truth? Go find out. If that means a trip to the school to see if your child is cutting classes, a room search to find drug items, or a phone call to the boyfriend's parents to find out what time they really came in, then do it. For those behaviors we have chosen as important, we must do whatever it takes to ensure that they are done. When children and teenagers find that they cannot manipulate us the way they used to, they have less temptation to lie.

Clear directions are a necessity in regaining control. The areas of a child's life where you are still in charge must be spelled out for you, your spouse, and your child. The child may try arguing, forgetting, lying, dawdling, throwing things, and leaving the house in order to detract you from what you really want—a specific behavior. These detractors are a problem; they are designed to get you, the parent, off the subject and on to something else. But remember, you want the behavior!

Are you willing to do whatever it takes to get your child to stop taking drugs, to go back to school, or to stop hitting his little sister? You need to be truly willing in order to get a change in behavior!

# 7

# The Biggest Hurdle
# in Parenting

The story is told in many first-year psychology classes about the retired psychologist who successfully practiced what he preached. It seems that several older children played in front of his house at the same time each day. Of course, the time coincided with his nap. After repeated efforts of asking the children to play elsewhere, the psychologist decided to pay the children a quarter apiece to play for one hour in the same spot at the same time each day. The children were delighted! What could be better than playing and getting paid for it?

Two days later the elderly man told the kids he was very sorry, but he had to reduce their pay to only 15 cents an hour. The children reacted with some disappointment, but agreed to continue on. Two more days passed of "playing for pay." The gentleman then told the kids that he had to further reduce their pay to just five cents an hour. The children couldn't believe it. Five cents an hour! In disgust they shouted, "That's not worth it—we're leaving!" Psychologist 1, kids 0.

Psychologists have known for decades that *all behavior has a goal and a payoff.* To increase your child's behavior toward a goal, you provide reinforcement, such as candy, tokens, TV time, money, a trip to Disneyland, an overnight stay at a friend's house, praise and recognition, or a month's supply of Twinkies! Initially, the worthwhile goal is not what causes the child to do the behavior; the reward of candy or money strengthens the behavior. But as the child grows and matures, his rewards become less tangible and more intrinsic. A better grade in science becomes worth more than five dollars for every "A" and three dollars for every "B."

Even as adults, our behavior has a purpose and a payoff. We work at jobs for pay, promotion, recognition, and achievement. Relationships with friends provide us with companionship, aid, understanding, and emotional support. *Everything you and I do has a goal and a payoff!* Writing this book is my goal. The payoff is the good feeling of accomplishment, the increased exposure to the public, the knowledge that I am helping parents raise their children, and, of course, the royalties!

Problems with children occur when *our* goal clashes with *their* goal. Would they rather watch TV or do homework? Play with their friends or clean up their room? You want this and they want that; the battle lines are drawn and the fight begins.

Besides having a clear goal and following through, another key ingredient in regaining control is *consistency: What is true today must also be true tomorrow.* Psychologists have found that when a behavior is rewarded every time it happens, people tend to lose interest and get bored and complacent. However, if a behavior is *never* rewarded, it will not last. The strongest type of behavior is the one that is inconsistently reinforced. For example, each year billions of dollars are gambled away by people hoping to hit it big. Gambling is a prime example of an *inconsistent or variable* reward system. Additional examples of behaviors that are rewarded inconsistently are fishing, dating, and yelling at children.

A friend of mine once said that his wife was a "four-no mother."

"What does that mean?" I asked.

"Well, it means that when she wants the kids to do something, she has to say it four times. Each time her voice gets a little louder and harsher. The fifth time she explodes!"

"So the kids know they have four no's to go before Mount Saint Helens erupts," I joked.

"Yup! They have her pegged!" he agreed.

The ultimate reward, even more than money, food, tokens, and making Mom pull her hair out, is *to be able to do whatever we want to do whenever and wherever we want to do it.* When children are inconsistently rewarded by getting their way, they will keep trying to get their way again and again.

If you have a six-year-old son who is playing outside and you have to tell him four times to come in for dinner, he has been conditioned by you to know that "I have four warnings until I must go in." You have inconsistently rewarded him before, so now he'll keep trying to see if he can avoid coming in right away for dinner.

A 15-year-old girl who has to be told five times to get off the phone knows she has four times to go after the first telling before she must get off the phone.

Children with parents who are irregular in enforcing some or all of the rules know they don't have to obey Mom or Dad yet. Children continue to play the odds and push their behavior to the limit to see if they can get their own way.

Do you want to encourage your children to misbehave? Then inconsistently enforce the rules of the house. Let them get by on some rules, delay on others, and develop "convenient amnesia" on still others. Kids will do everything they can to make you inconsistent when it works to their advantage.

## COMMON REASONS FOR PARENTAL INCONSISTENCY

Your rules can be crystal-clear and your follow-through can be effective at getting the job done, yet the biggest hurdle that parents face time and time again is *consistency*! If there is one ingredient that will make or break your control, this is it. By not being consistent in enforcing a rule, you are giving your child the key to the parental slot machine. Why is it so difficult to be consistent? Let's look at several reasons.

## The Chip Shot

This is one I hear from coast to coast: "My daughter will ask to go out at the last minute. I'll say 'No, you have homework to do.' Then she'll say, 'But I don't have any.' Then I'll reply with, 'No, you were out last night. Two nights in a row is too much.' She will hit me with, 'But my friends get to do it! You never let me go out! You don't care!' Then I will begin to get angry and hurt and will shoot back, 'You get to do lots of things. I work hard to be a good parent to you, and you don't appreciate it!' The argument continues, covering my parenting skills, fairness, all the other kids in the school, grades, Dad, curfew, my gestapo tactics, and so on. Finally I give in because I can't take it anymore. I feel beaten."

The *chip shot* is a child's repeated effort to wear the parent down. Children seem to know when Mom and Dad are at their weakest—just after work, during the folding of five loads of laundry, in the middle of a good soap opera, or while Mom has the flu. It's like a waterfall hitting a rock for centuries; eventually the rock wears down!

All children try to wear down their parents. They know our breaking points. Do they do this to be mean? Not usually. They do it to get their own way.

Here are some suggestions to keep the rock from wearing down. First, make sure your children and teenagers know the rules of the house and can repeat them clearly and accurately. For example, a rule for your 15-year-old daughter might be "You may go out once a week during school nights in addition to Bible study. Your grade average must be maintained at a 2.5

level to keep this privilege. You may not be gone longer than three hours and must be home by 9:30." Ask your youngster what her understanding of the rule is. When she can demonstrate to you that she understands what you want and the implications of breaking the rule, you have taken a big step forward in regaining control. If your rules are clear and concise, then your child must fight with the rule, not you.

Second, tell your child or teenager that you will never make decisions when you first walk in the door from work, shopping, or whatever. You need a few minutes to unload, freshen up, get some coffee, or merely breathe for five minutes. Yes, sometimes decisions must be made right away, but if you possibly can, avoid that rush of pressure when you hit the doorway. *That's a good ambush tactic that kids use!* By giving yourself time to decide or to enforce a rule, it teaches them that you have needs too—to rest, unwind, relieve yourself, unpack, and breathe. In addition, the kids must learn to plan their schedules better, to make those phone calls themselves that would answer your questions of who, when, where, why, and how much. This teaches them that Mom and Dad are not going to let them off the hook; they must take personal responsibility for certain things if they want them badly enough.

## A Prisoner in Disguise

Parents often complain that when their child is in the house on restriction, they are prisoners as well. When a rule is consistently enforced, kids will sometimes try to make Mom and Dad pay for it. Door-slamming, silence, tears, throwing things, a sloppy room cleanup, or semi-clean dishes all make life unbearable for Mom and Pop. And this strategy works! "The punishment to us is worse than the discipline to him" parents exclaim. When parents give in to these tantrums, they might as well be giving the child quarters for the slot machine! Yes, it's tough to put up with a pouty child or teen (I don't know where it's guaranteed that parenting will ever be easy), but our responsibility as parents is to "train up," to teach children that life has many lessons to learn about behavior and responsibility. If the kids don't begin to learn this fact at home, they will get thrown for a loop out in the world. After all, how many times will your son's boss at work put up with lateness, sloppy work, or a poor attitude?

The next time you enforce a rule and consistently follow through on it, ask yourself if this is a rule worth battling over. If the answer is yes, then the real issue becomes "Who's in charge here?" You'd better be willing to "go to the mat" enforcing a rule you have determined is worth fighting for. That might include some nights or weekends spent at home enforcing a curfew. With persistence, the kids will get the message that you mean business.

This reminds me of one of the most popular teachers at the junior high school where I taught for a few years. Her motto was "Be fair, but sit on 'em hard the first three months and then you can coast the rest of the year." If anyone needed clear and concise rules, effective follow-through, and persistence, it was me during my first year of teaching. Not only was I unsure of what my rules were, but my need for the students' approval would have weakened any guidelines I set up anyway. This teacher's motto came to mean a lot to me, for it allowed me to enjoy teaching instead of fearing and despising it.

Your children desperately need to know what is important to you, what your values are, and how willing you are to fight for what is important. If it is a clean room, then stick to it. If you have decided instead to give that area over to your son or daughter, then your only battle is one of personal restraint! Again, *choose your battles wisely!*

## The Nice Guy

Parenting takes courage and a healthy measure of self-esteem. Saying no and enforcing a rule is difficult at best. We all want our children to like us, yet we pay a price for thinking "They must like me," "I need their approval," or "The kids have to be happy with everything I do as a parent." If these are your thoughts, you have become a prisoner of faulty thinking. As a result, how your kids react to what you say and do affects how consistently you enforce your rules. It becomes a vicious cycle: 1) The parent enforces a rule and follows through; 2) the child reacts with hurt, tears, anger, silence, threats, and/or accusations; 3) the parent reacts to the child's response with feelings of disapproval, inadequacy, fear, hurt, anger, or sadness; 4) the parent then alters the original plan to follow through and be consistent. At this point the parent either gets angry and attacks, feels hurt and withdraws, or becomes fearful and does nothing. Reactions might include giving in through backing off on the rule ("Okay, but just this once"), buying the child something (bribery), or responding *like* the child by crying, getting angry, slamming doors, yelling, and so on ("Well, you hurt me too!").

The good news is that you don't have to respond this way. If you are a prisoner of your child's approval, it's time to break free from this cell. As parents we get in the trap of *needing* our children's love and approval. To give your children the right to stamp "okay" or "not okay" on your behavior puts *them* in control, not you.

"I *must* have my child's okay on my decisions"; "The teenagers *have to* like the rules I want to enforce or I can't follow through"; "They *ought to* want to obey me or I've failed to gain their respect." Are such self-talk beliefs holding onto you? Release them! Who said your children *must* like everything you do? Where is it etched in stone that "children *must* agree that the rules of the house are all completely fair"? Where does the belief come from that says you've failed miserably as a parent if the children and teenagers don't obey every time you ask them to?

Being a parent in control is to risk not being liked all the time. *Our parenting is geared to what the children need, not what they want.* Think about that statement. If God gave us all we wanted, we would be in bigger trouble than we often are!

## Saying No to Myself

If you are like most Americans, you have at least one or two credit cards. And, if you fit the typical profile, these cards are almost up to their credit limit! Advertisers know that our culture spawns a "want-it-now" philosophy, and they play this to the hilt. Easy deals, fast food, and quick dry all lead to a kind of "microwave mentality." This affects our parenting as well: We want advice from a nice thin book that gives simple answers. The directives in the book must work the first time or else we'll buy another book.

Why is it so difficult to say no to our children when we feel we must? First of all, we often want their approval. To give them a negative answer is to risk their anger, rejection, and punishment. So much of our own identity is tied up in our children. When they hurt, we hurt—and we want to fix it. When the children are angry, we can't bear to let them work through the anger, but instead change the rules to prevent their wrath. What parents fail to realize is that the kids are reacting to the "no" more than to the parent. Yet Mom and Dad feel a personal rebuff. What is at issue is *the principle which the "no" is trying to teach*, not our identity. If our child's reaction to limit-setting causes us to back off, bend the rules, or set fewer and fewer boundaries, then we have a case of "credit-card parentitis." We need to deal with the principle, not the pressure!

Another reason it's difficult to say no to our kids is that our parents either did not set limits for us or set them too tight. Think about it for a minute. Who was the disciplinarian in your family as you grew up? Did you have too much freedom or not enough? I find that it's common for parents to not want their children to react to them as they did to their parents. When a mother says, "My dad was way too strict; I had to sneak out at night in order to go anywhere," she often sets too few limits. She doesn't want her kids to resent her as she did her father. Yet she doesn't understand why her children are so out of control.

Still other parents tighten the noose and don't let their children grow and assume more responsibility. Their own parents set few rules, were never around, or acted like the children were invisible. "I want my children to know I care, that I am involved in their lives," they say. This parent does not want his children to feel neglected and abandoned. The boundaries he sets are a way of showing that fact.

Do you find that it's difficult to hand over more responsibility to your child as he or she grows up? We must remember that parenting is moving from control of the child's life to influence in later years. The trust you place in your child to do what's best and make the right choices is showing love in the strongest possible way. Sure, he won't always make the right choices initially. That's one way kids learn. *You've got to gain freedom from your child so that he can gain his own freedom from you.*

## The Case of the Messy Room

In the many seminars and classes I've conducted on parenting, the number one problem that parents report is how to handle the dilemma of the messy room. This seems to be where the battle lines are clearly drawn. Some of the cries of battle-weary parents are: "Clean it up or I'll have to hose it down"; "If you don't get that room in order I'll lock you in it and feed you through a knothole"; or "I give up! I'll just give you a year's supply of Roach Motels." Instead of a desperate, last-minute summit meeting with your child, let's look at a possible solution.

Mom says to her son as he's watching television, "Your room looks messy. When are you going to clean it up?"

"In a few minutes, Mom, after this show is over," he replies with the utmost sincerity in his voice.

Having asked him to clean his room, the mother goes about her business of fixing dinner.

From your experience as a parent, what do you think will happen?

## Questions

1. Have the parents decided that the room is the boy's problem or their own? When, at what age, will it be only *his* problem?
2. Did Mom *direct* the boy to clean the room or merely ask a question?
3. Is the boy likely to get right up at this point and clean his room? Was Mom concerned that the job be done now or later?
4. Did the mother follow through and see to it that the boy cleaned his room *at that time*?
5. Will the mother have to tell the boy again? How many more times would you guess?

As Mom pokes her head out of the kitchen she sees her son still watching television. "Let's go, get that room clean!" she shouts.

"Okay, Mom, the show is almost over," he replies.

"Well, get right to it when this is over." Mom pulls her head back into the kitchen and continues preparing dinner.

## Questions

1. Do you think the boy will jump up right now because of Mom's increased vocal command?
2. Has she yet directed the boy to clean his room *now*?
3. Did the mother follow through to see that the room was cleaned *now*?
4. Will the mom have to tell the boy again?

As the mother is finishing up the meal, she notices that the television is still on. She feels a shot of anger cut through her, storms out into the family room, and shouts, "I thought I told you to clean up that room!"

"You did, but after this is over!" he shouts back.

"I don't think this is the show you were watching when I first asked you to clean your room. I'm sick of you taking advantage of me! Get going and clean that room!"

"Quit yelling! I was just going to do it. You're always yelling at me to do things. I have to do more around here than anybody else! It isn't fair!"

"Fair?" she sputters in return. "Let me tell you about fair!"

Now they're off and running. Tempers are flying, as often happens when parents get put off and have to bring in the big stick.

What are the key ingredients in regaining control?

1. *Decide who owns the problem.* Is the responsibility yours or the child's? If it is his, let go of it. Why fight over what you've already given over to the child or teen? Remember: *Pick your battles wisely or you'll be battling all the time!*
2. *Are your rules clear and concise*, with words that tell when, where, how much, how often, and how well?
3. *Are you willing to follow through* and make sure that the responsibility is finished?
4. *Is the rule the same yesterday, today, and tomorrow?*

Let's look at the same scene again, this time with the principles described above put into action. First, the mother has decided the son must clean his room. She and her son have worked out the agreement that he is to clean it once per week, Saturday mornings by 10 o'clock. There are to be no exceptions. She has drawn her battle line at this point.

Second, the standards for how well the room should be cleaned have been defined. With some kids this is not a problem, but with others you have to spell it all out: how to make the bed, where to put the clothes, what to do with the dishes, and where to hide the cockroaches.

Now it is Saturday morning at 10:15. The son is watching the Smurfs.

"Aaron, it is Saturday morning at 10:15. Your room is not clean as we had agreed. Turn the television off and clean your room *now.*"

"Just wait until 10:30. Then the show will be over."

The mother walks over to the television set and turns it off. She then steps over to him and says, "What is your understanding of the rule we set up together about cleaning your room?"

"To clean it on Saturdays," he says.

"What else do you understand about the rule?" she asks.

"I have to clean it by 10 o'clock."

"Right. So get up and clean your room now." He promptly finds he has an official escort to his room.

The boy knows he has no choice. The mother will stay with him until he cleans his room. The rule is not optional; it is mandatory. Every Saturday morning that the room is not cleaned by 10 o'clock the same thing will happen. If he is outside, she will go and get him. If he is staying over at someone's house and has not cleaned it beforehand or made special arrangements, he will have to come home to clean it. The point is this: *The parent is in control of the battles that he or she has chosen to fight.*

Once you have worked this out with your spouse and with each of your children, and you are convinced that their perception of the rule is the same as yours, then the biggest hurdle you'll face is inconsistency. The more you are persistent in enforcing your rules, the less effort you will need in the future.

# 8

# Which Type of Discipline?

Recently a good friend of mine purchased a new mini-van. As we were taking it for a ride he began playing with a variety of buttons, switches, and levers. "I just can't seem to figure out how to work all these things," he complained.

"Have you read through the owner's manual yet?" I asked.

"Who has time? I never read those things, though I probably should. Once I built a bike backward because I didn't want to look at all the instructions."

If you are like most parents, your tendency is to not "read the instructions" until your kids get out of hand.

Only then do you look for guidance from books, seminars, counselors, TV talk shows, tapes, radio programs, best friends, and even your own children. One single mother of four teenage daughters told me she often asked one or two of her girls for advice on discipline matters that concerned the other daughters. "I know if I don't find out from them what I should do, they'll get angry and say I'm not being fair."

As if needing help were not stressful enough, sifting through the mixed bag of discipline methods adds to our anxiety level. We hear about logical consequences, natural consequences, "freedom to fail," rewards and reinforcements, extinction, behavioral contracts, shaping behavior techniques, time out, "I messages," and anything else that some expert claims works best for every kid on the block. The fact is that each of these methods has its place. The problem is which ones to choose, and for what behaviors.

You might be surprised to learn that all of these methods have much in common. Let's look at a common thread that ties them all together, then examine the two most widely talked about and used methods—logical-and-natural-consequences and reinforcement/reward.

## THE TIE THAT BINDS

All discipline methods have one thing in common—the issue of control. Where does control come from? Power. And where does power come from? Authority. Jesus had all the power He needed at His fingertips, yet He taught with authority and didn't need to use the power. People knew He was powerful just by His author-itative manner. In the same way parents start out hav-ing authority and control. They have it because they control the infant's life. If they didn't, a child would never survive.

As children grow, the authority of the parents often begins to erode. Somehow the kids gain power and control. They feel they have the authority to tell Mom and Dad what to do. You know the type of child; she says she is "eight going on 25." When kids misbehave, they are exercising their power and control, doing what they want to do. You must decide who is the authority in your family and who has the power and control. You are the parent and therefore you are the authority.

All methods of discipline share the concept of con-trol, but they use different methods. The key is that you, the parent, decide how the control is deployed. *This is a critical factor.* When I decide to let my son be in charge of his skateboard, and don't constantly remind him that he has left it outside, I have given him control. The responsibility is now his. I have not given up; I have simply given that area over to him. The one who is in control has the authority to let go; he can delegate his power. This is the way the military operates. A sergeant is given authority over new recruits. If he takes the responsibility before it is given to him, there is a serious problem! His commanding officers make sure that he is trained and ready before giving him command of a unit. It works the same way in parenting.

The concept of letting go of your children as they grow and mature rests on this principle. Control over children's lives is handed over to them as they develop the capacity to use it. To develop this capacity they need to experiment with a measure of personal responsibility. This too is given. When my son first got his skateboard, the rule was clear: It is not to be left outside after dark. The privilege of using the skateboard was linked to his ability to bring it in each night. After a proving time, *he was given charge* over the skateboard. And wouldn't you know it—he left it out one night and it was stolen! Mom and Dad let go of the job of reminding him to bring it in after he proved he could handle it. Sadly for him, one slipup cost him a lot.

We believed he was capable of caring for the skateboard. We still believe it. He made a mistake and paid a price. Our message to him was not "See, we told you so" or "How could you do that after we paid so much money for that board?" Instead, our message was "We believe you can still take care of your things. You are capable."

Over the parenting years, the continuing question is: Who is responsible for my child's behavior? What areas is he in charge of and what areas am I still responsible for? No method of discipline will help you until you begin to answer this question. It will keep you on track as you gain freedom from your child so that he can gain his freedom from you. Actually, as your kids get older they will remind you that you need to let go with statements such as "Will you quit running my life!"

With that in mind, let's look at several methods of discipline. Then in the next chapter, we'll walk through a number of common trouble spots for parents and see how the different techniques might work.

## LOGICAL AND NATURAL CONSEQUENCES

Logical consequences let the positive and negative results of a child's actions teach him a lesson. This allows several things to happen: 1) It gets parents out of the picture and frees us from fights, nagging, and confrontations; 2) the child is taught accountability and responsibility for his own decisions, indecisions, actions, and inactions; and 3) a power struggle is avoided because the child has to argue with himself; he made the decision and is accountable for it personally (even though he might try to pin it on Mom or Dad).

The idea of a consequence being logical is very important. In order for it to work, *it must be logical to your child.* Putting your teenage daughter on restriction because she did not put away her dirty clothes is not logical. Letting her do her own wash for a week makes sense. When a five-year-old boy smears finger paint on the bathroom wall, putting him to bed early without dinner is not logical. Giving him a small bucket of soapy water and a sponge to clean the mess makes sense. I have listed a few additional situations and some consequences below. See which consequences or combinations of consequences make sense to you:

1. *Behavior:* David, age nine, continually leaves his skateboard out each night after dark.

*Consequences:* Threaten to saw it in half with a chain saw; let it stay out until it gets stolen; yell at him for his irresponsibility and then put it away yourself; put him to bed early; restrict him from using the skateboard for a period of time and help him develop a system so *he* can remember to put it away.

2. *Behavior:* Amy, age 14, sneaks into Mom's cosmetic case and uses her makeup.

*Consequences:* Sneak into her room and retrieve your makeup; lecture her about being too young for makeup; put a lock on the case or bathroom door; charge her a "makeup fee" for using the cosmetics and take it out of her allowance; find out what she likes about Mom's makeup and work with her on getting the same type for her own case.

3. *Behavior:* Jennifer, age five, repeatedly leaves her toys on the living room floor.

*Consequences:* Leave them there forever and hope she gets the idea; make her sit in the corner until she decides to pick them up; threaten to sell them all at the next garage sale; put the toys away and restrict her from their use for a period of time (evening, day, week).

4. *Behavior:* Jim, age seven, is often 15 minutes late for dinner.

*Consequences:* Make him wash the dishes; let him eat cold food; send him away without dinner; let him prepare his own dinner.

5. *Behavior:* Sharon, age 16, watches TV every night and doesn't start her homework until 10 P.M.

*Consequences:* Try to convince her that she'll grow up to be a good-for-nothing if she doesn't do her homework; lock her in her room until she does the homework; unplug the TV; use the "when-then" principle (when she does an hour of homework then she gets an hour of TV); let her experience the consequences of poor homework performance (bad grades, notes from teachers, embarrassment).

As you read over the five behavior problems, which consequences seemed to logically apply to the behavior? Those that provide choices and develop responsibility are the ones to use.

In problem number one, what consequences would teach David responsibility for his skateboard? David's behavior indicates that he either doesn't care about his skateboard, knows Mom or Dad will get it for him, or has a difficult time remembering to pick it up. Rather than sawing it in half or yelling, allow the board to get stolen (better for older kids) or else restrict him from using the board for a period of time (and help him develop a system to remember to put it away). One of these two options would be the consequence to choose.

In problem number two, Amy's sneaking into Mom's cosmetic case could mean that she wants to be more like Mom and needs to spend time with her in this area. Or perhaps she is protesting her parents' unwillingness to allow her to grow up and begin to wear certain types of makeup. Or she might feel that whatever is Mom's is also hers. Usually when girls do this, though, it's because they want Mom to help them learn more about growing up. They need the attention that only Mom can give. A natural consequence would be to spend time with the daughter, teaching her and shopping with her for makeup. Perhaps taking a makeup class together would be a good idea. If the problem persists, either locking the makeup case or charging her a "fee" for using the makeup would be additional consequences.

The third problem concerns Jennifer leaving her toys in the living room. The most logical consequence for this, after making efforts to get her to pick them up, is to gather the toys into a bag and tell her she will not have these to play with for one day. This might also be a time for Mom or Dad to play games with her, read a book to her, or make a project together. The consequence should be *not playing with the toys* rather than restriction from Mom or Dad.

Jim's lateness for dinner, problem number four, could be due to the fact that he doesn't know what time dinner is, or the inconsistency of the dinnertime, or the chance to make a grand entrance. A logical consequence would be for him to eat a cold dinner. If he misses dinner, he either goes without or makes his own, provided he cleans up after himself.

Situation number five, Sharon's constant TV-watching, is certainly a problem to be concerned about. Her unwillingness to do homework could be due to a learning problem which has not been detected, classes that are too difficult for her (which might indicate a need for a tutor or a transfer to easier classes), depression, boredom, or just plain unconcern. The most logical consequence is to not allow television until the homework is finished. Often parents don't know if there is homework to be done. The often-heard "We didn't have any" or "I did it in class" really means "I want to watch TV and I don't want to do homework." Checking with teachers by phone or in conference, getting progress reports on a weekly basis, and reviewing the homework each night are good places to start. It's very important to stay on top of this problem because it is so easy to get behind and get caught in a spiral of failure.

When you decide to use logical consequences, several issues must be very clear. First, present consequences as choices. Choices within limits provide a child with the opportunity to learn to make good decisions. For example:

"Either put your toys away in the proper place each night by bedtime or else I will lock them up for one week."

"You can either feed the dog on a regular basis each night by 7 P.M. or else I will give it away when you miss more than once per week."

"Your dirty clothes go in the hamper in the bathroom each morning before you leave for school or else they will not get washed. You will then have to wash them yourself for seven days."

Remember, you are letting the child choose, so be sure you can live with his decision. *If you can't, then don't give him a choice!*

Second, follow through if your child chooses the consequence instead of what you asked him to do. If you do not follow through, then he learns another consequence: "Mom or Dad inconsistently follow through, so I can play the odds." Remember the slot-machine principle!

Third, include your children in the creation of the consequences. Make it something you do *with* them, not *to* them. For example, you might say to your 15-year-old daughter, "Sarah, I have a problem with the way you leave your dirty clothes on the floor each morning for me to pick up and wash. I get angry about it, but I realize it's your problem, not mine. I'm going to make some changes in this routine. Do you have any solutions to this problem?" If Sarah can't think of something then or at a later time, then you can let her know, "Beginning today, I will leave your dirty clothes on the floor and let you begin to do your own wash for seven days. After that maybe we can come up with a better plan." At the end of the seven days, find out what your youngster has thought of to solve the dilemma. If the child can participate in the creation of the rule and the consequence, she is much more likely to follow through on it herself.

Fourth, don't say "I told you so!" Let the consequences speak for themselves. When you give a child responsibility in an area, let him deal with the consequences without your sideline interference. He is more likely to talk with you about what happened if he doesn't see you snickering with delight.

Natural consequences differ from logical ones in that they are results that you and your child have not planned in advance. They result from letting the child or teenager experience the reality of life. If you touch a hot stove, you get burned. When your child refuses to eat lunch, he gets to listen to his stomach growl. The boy who doesn't want to wear his jacket outside will soon come back in when it's too cold. The girl who continually puts down one of her friends will soon experience the consequence of having one less friend, or maybe no friends and a bad reputation!

Underlying the use of consequences is the question "What do I want my child to learn from this freedom of choice?" Being a parent in control means knowing those areas in which you are letting the child experience the results of his action. In addition, *you are in control* of those areas which the child cannot control. For example, you cannot let a three-year-old experience the natural consequences of running into the street or hitting his sister with a bat. Such actions could prove disastrous. However, he could learn to get ready for bed *before* having a story, watching TV, eating a snack, or getting more playtime. A parent could say something like "John, it's 7 o'clock. Bedtime is at 7:30. When the buzzer goes off you are to get your pajamas on. When you have your pajamas on, then you may have a snack before bed and story time."

As your child grows, his areas of choice expand and your areas of control diminish. You will feel much more comfortable with this natural change in parenting if your children are allowed choices from their earliest years. Begin to give them some freedom now! A few of the main areas in which you might consider giving a child more freedom include:

1. Bedtime
2. Money
3. Curfew
4. Homework time
5. Phone time
6. Television time
7. Choice of household chores at 7:30
8. Cleaning up the bedroom
9. Choice of friends
10. Putting toys away

## REINFORCEMENTS AND REWARDS

John B. Watson, an often-quoted behavioral psychologist of the early twentieth century, boasted, "Give me a dozen healthy infants and I'll guarantee to take any one at random and train him to be a doctor, lawyer, artist, merchant, beggarman, or thief." While this claim may be somewhat overstated, much behavior is shaped by the consequences it produces. If the results of someone's action can be "engineered," then his behavior can be shaped. Even as a pigeon can be conditioned to peck a button for some corn, so also a child's actions are reinforced when he learns that if he cries long enough after being put to bed, someone will come and give him a drink of water. *When a behavior is followed by a reinforcer, the behavior is strengthened.*

When you stop and think about it, you and I receive reinforcers all the time. Praise, a hug, attention, a wink, a smile, a touch, and a pat on the back are all examples of what is known as "social reinforcers." These are the most powerful reinforcers because they are found in the behaviors of other people. They cost nothing to give and occur hundreds of times each day. You reinforce your child when he talks to you and you give him direct eye contact coupled with a smile. This tells him you want to listen and encourages him to share with you. When you begin to look away, read the newspaper, watch TV, yawn, or fall asleep, the positive message you were sending stops. The child is no longer receiving a positive reinforcer from you. If he wants the attention badly enough, he might turn off the TV, grab your newspaper, yell, cry, or get into trouble. Sometimes my son David will do what his preschool teacher did to him—put his hand underneath my chin and turn my head to look directly at him. This shows what powerful reinforcement my attention is to him!

Tangible reinforcers are things such as money, food, prizes, points or gold stars on a chart, more TV time, a night's stay with a friend, use of the phone, and a later curfew. These are what you use in making contracts or charts with children. There are specific behaviors that you want to see happen and specific rewards for the child to work toward. For example, suppose an eight-year-old boy is to clean up his room every morning before school. He gets one gold star for making the bed, a star for putting his dirty clothes in the hamper, and another star for picking up his toys. He checks off on a chart the number of stars he received that day. At the end of the week the stars are totaled, with a maximum of 21 stars per week. These can be traded for money, food, toys, TV time, playtime, or whatever the child wants most.

Younger children need reinforcement daily. You might want to "trade in" the points, stars, tokens, or play money on a daily or even per-job basis for reinforcements such as candy, TV time, or playtime with Dad. Older children can total the points each day and wait until Saturday for payday!

In using both social and tangible reinforcements with children, you must keep several points in mind.

1. *When a behavior is followed by a reinforcer, the behavior is strengthened.* This means that the behavior is more likely to occur again if it is followed by something the child likes. My small daughter likes popsicles, books, candy, and hand-clapping as rewards. She responds excitedly to these rewards. As Amy grows, the nature of the reinforcers will change from popsicles to going to the movies, a new blouse, or more time on the telephone. What do your children respond positively to (not what do you want them to respond to)? How are

your reactions to their present behavior shaping (reinforcing) future behavior? Remember, social reinforcers,
the most powerful tools you have, cost little to give and
take just a second or two!

2. *Target a specific behavior.* If your goal is to have your
child become more polite, you must know what "polite"
means, for it means different things to different people. Instead of telling your son "Webster, be more
polite next time," identify one or more parts of politeness to work on. Saying "thank you," "please," and
"excuse me," holding the door open for other people,
and offering to help carry in the groceries for Mom all
make up politeness. How will your child know when he
or she is doing what you want if you haven't been
specific? When will you know to give him a gold star for
being "polite" if you don't know specifically what behaviors you want?

Another often-heard example of a vague goal is
"Have a good attitude." What does that mean? Having
a "good attitude" should be broken down into specific
behaviors, such as closing the door gently even when
angry, not using certain words, no name-calling, only
positive comments about the dinner (if any), taking out
the trash without a monologue on reinstating child
labor laws, and keeping hands and feet off of little
sister. If target behaviors are not specific and broken
down into component parts, the child is overwhelmed.
One 38-year-old man I saw in therapy often referred to
the time when he was eight and his father told him to
go downstairs and clean the basement. He went down
and sat for an hour, not knowing where to start or what
"clean" meant to his father.

Another word for targeting behavior is "pinpointing." If you can't describe it or count it, then you aren't being specific enough. Observe your child and count the number of times he does a certain behavior each day. Try to work on something your child does five times or more a day. If you want to eliminate teasing little sister, observe what happens for a couple of days to see exactly what big brother does to her. Write these behaviors on a list and tape the list on the refrigerator so *both* of you can see it. You should also pinpoint the opposite behaviors. In other words, what is it that you want him to do instead of teasing? "Share toys," "Watch TV for 30 minutes without fighting," and "Play quietly for ten minutes with little sister" are examples. You can then set up two columns on a chart: one for "teasing" and the other for "happy faces." At the end of the day the happy faces could be exchanged for something special.

3. *Reinforce immediately and often.* When you see a behavior you like, reinforce it! A complaint I often hear when counseling couples is that the husband never compliments his wife. He says in defense, "I do think about how nice you look. I just never say it." It doesn't do any good to just *think* about reinforcing behavior; you have to actually *do* it.

Some parents feel that if they reinforce the child too much, he will be spoiled: "He should behave because that's what children are supposed to do." The idea behind this is that we should not enjoy or get any gratification out of things we are supposed to do. I call this the General Patton style of parenting.

No matter what the child does, he should get something, even if it is as simple as a smile or a wink. You don't have to go out and buy him a new motorcycle! The rule of thumb to remember is: *If a desirable behavior occurs, reinforce it!* In one sense we cannot not reinforce; even if we do nothing, that is reinforcing in a negative way.

4. *Establish a point value for each behavior.* Some kids pick up behaviors by responding to social reinforcers such as hugs, kisses, smiles, and "thank you's." Others need additional rewards in order to learn new behaviors. For example, when an eight-year-old daughter takes her plate to the sink after finishing dinner, what is the reinforcement for that behavior? If the social reinforcements don't seem to be enough, then give the behavior a point value: one point for taking her plate, one for her glass, one for the silverware, and five for wiping off the table. Or instead of points you could use play money, tokens, gold stars, or beans. With older children (nine and up) it's fun to use astronomical numbers, such as 5000 points for brushing your teeth before 9 P.M. or 50,000 "squeegies" for making your bed before school. It adds humor to the system and makes it fun. Children can even help design and make the play money, tokens, chips, or stars.

Charting and point systems are ideal methods to get new behaviors going. You'll find that after a while the behaviors will just happen and the child will not be looking for the reward as readily. At first he will remind you of the star, token, gum, or story. Later on you'll be reminding him! This will tell you he has learned the behavior and no longer needs the specific reward you have worked out. However, this is not to say that he doesn't need a social reinforcer of some kind.

5. *Reinforce small steps toward the goal.* How do you teach a child to "be more polite," "be a good student," or "keep your room clean"? If you were to wait until his room is completely clean before you reinforced him, it would never happen. Instead, work on small steps toward the goal of cleaning the room. To do this you have to break down the job into bite-size behaviors. (Older kids can obviously take bigger bites.) In the example above of the girl cleaning off the table, the job was broken down into behaviors such as taking her dish, glass, and silverware to the sink and wiping off the table. If cleaning the bedroom consists of making the bed, picking up the clothes, and putting away the toys, start with only one of the behaviors. Toddlers can learn to put their toys into a toy box, on shelves, in bins, or in a special place set aside for toys. In our house we had pictures of the toys taped down on the shelves so that each toy (or type of toy, like cars) had its place. This made the job more precise and less complicated. We knew when the job was done and how well it was accomplished.

*It is important to realize what the child can and cannot do.* You must start where his or her ability dictates. A toddler cannot make his bed, but he can help by putting his pillow on the bed or placing his stuffed animals on the pillow. He can also begin to put toys away and set napkins on the table. Be creative! Ask other parents what their kids are doing, and build on these ideas.

6. *Use the "when-then" principle.* Most children respond to social reinforcers such as praise, touch, attention, and smiles. These are simple things and occur dozens of times each day. If any one of these responses

consistently follows a child's behavior, then that behavior is likely to occur again in the future. Some children are less responsive to these social rewards than are others. Parents of such children need to implement a program of behavior change that includes the tangible reinforcers, such as riding the bike, playing outside, no chores for the evening, or more time on the computer.

The "when-then" principle simply tells the child, "*When* you hang up your clothes *then* you can go outside" or "*When* you take two bites of peas *then* you can have dessert." You must be sure to link something the child wants with the behavior you want. "When you take your dishes to the sink then you get to do your homework" doesn't sound too appetizing!

Rewards and reinforcers are powerful tools to use in getting our children and teenagers to do what we want them to do. As they grow, the characteristics of the rewards change, as does our ability to control the behaviors of the youngster. Reinforcers for teenagers shift more and more to outside the family, leaving the parents with less leverage. Social rewards such as time with friends, use of the phone, getting a job, using the car, and going to spend the night at someone's house become more desirable and powerful. You are not able to give most of the reinforcers as you once were, but you still have some control.

7. *Use "Time Out" as a discipline tool.* The "discipline" used by most of us often consists of yelling, scolding, nagging, crying, and the silent treatment. The problem is that most of the time these methods don't work. "You are a selfish brat! Now stop taking your brother's toy!" may be effective for a few minutes, but before you

know it the child is back at it again. Time out (TO) is a technique that works. After several days of consistent practice, you'll find that neither you nor your child are doing as much yelling at each other. It is generally useful for younger children, from three to eleven years old.

Time out is time away from positive reinforcement. It requires a place where there are no toys, no other people, and nothing to play with. The best place is usually the bathroom as long as it is well lighted and not frightening to the child. If TO hasn't worked in the past, chances are that you were: 1) inconsistent in using it, 2) did not use the bathroom, or 3) were not using a timing device that the child could hear (such as an egg timer). Research has shown that three minutes of TO works as well as 30 minutes. It is better if you use short time periods (two to five minutes) and stick with this system. Don't start at 20 minutes and then cut back.

Time out works well with fighting, teasing, whining, temper tantrums, arguing, and wandering off. It sounds easy to use, but it is not. You will find, though, that after consistent use it pays off in better-behaved children.

## REWARDS OR CONSEQUENCES?

By now you are probably wondering "What's the difference in these methods?" In reality, very little, yet much has been written about each approach. Let's look at them together.

First, both approaches say that you need to know what behavior you want the child to do and not do. Be specific; pinpoint target behaviors. Your child needs to know what you want, and so do you.

Second, each method relies on the consequences of one's actions. "Behavior is shaped by its consequences," say behaviorists; "Logical consequences teach children responsibility for their actions," say proponents of natural and logical consequences. In either case, what a child gets in return for his behavior either reinforces or does not reinforce his future behavior, whether it is called a reward or a logical consequence. With both discipline methods the child makes a choice and receives a reward or consequence for it.

The essential difference between the methods lies in the fact that the reward method uses a scientific approach to behavior change—observing, pinpointing, and counting behaviors; making a chart or contract; and setting up a reward system. The goal of changing behaviors is reached in planned increments, small steps toward the goal. This is the approach to use more often for younger children when you want to teach a *new behavior* that might seem too complex to master otherwise. By breaking down the behaviors into small steps, the child can be rewarded for accomplishing each step, with the end result being the completion of all of the steps in sequence. Bed-wetting, tantrums, whining, toilet training, setting the table, brushing teeth, taking a shower, going to bed, and doing homework are just a few of the behaviors that can be taught and reinforced with behavioral techniques. It's more work than using logical consequences, but the time spent will get the job done.

In contrast, the logical-and-natural-consequences method holds the child responsible for his behavior. It allows him to make choices presented to him by his parents and to then experience the result of those choices. The child who refuses to eat goes hungry; the boy who goes to bed late is tired and crabby the next day. The essential purpose of allowing natural consequences and designing logical consequences is to encourage children to make responsible choices. Let them choose and be accountable for the choice, whether it turns out well or not.

When you want to teach new, complex behaviors, a reinforcement system works best. As the child grows and his repertoire of behaviors and abilities increases, logical and natural consequences are more effective because they give more responsibility to the youngster. Since being a parent involves moving from control to influence, giving the child greater freedom of choice is the key to successful parenting. In the next chapter we will tackle a number of specific behavioral problems and demonstrate the principles we have been looking at.

# 9

# Putting It All Together

Sometimes I think the best psychologists in the world are children. They spend years training you to yell, drawing you into arguments, playing you against your spouse, slyly changing the subject, and getting you to procrastinate, forget, and finally give up. Well, now it's time to regain control of your behavior and take charge of theirs! This chapter will focus on problem behaviors using the principles we have discussed. If you follow the step-by-step procedures, you can immediately begin the process of retaking control. With every behavior you want to change, several decisions must be made.

1. *The behavior I want changed is* . . . Remember, you must deal with *specifics*. Pinpoint exactly what it is that you want changed: hitting little sister, taking out the trash, running away, cutting classes, staying in bed, or throwing temper tantrums on the floor. "Loving your fellowman" and "having a good attitude" aren't clear because they don't tell the child specifically what you want him or her to do.

2. *How might I be feeding the problem behavior?* Until we are clear about our own behavior, we will unwittingly contribute to the problem. Unclear rules or an absence of rules, inconsistent enforcement, no follow-through, yelling, screaming, hitting, giving up, and beliefs such as "It's an inherited behavior" or "He's just going through a stage" are examples of how we play a part in losing control. Ask for help from your spouse, a good friend, a teacher, or a relative to find out what you are doing to make matters worse, then begin today to change your own behavior!

3. *Will I give the child a choice or is the behavior a "must"?* Younger children have more "must" behaviors required of them than older kids. Examples of mandatory behaviors might include not running into the street, staying out of the medicine cabinet, making your bed daily, no wandering around the neighborhood, stop hitting baby brother, staying in school all day, and not using drugs or alcohol. With teenagers we may have less control, but we still have some! Choices use the words "when . . . then" and allow the child to choose whether to clean his room or stay indoors until it's done; come to the dinner table with clean hands or miss dinner; take out the trash or pay a service fee to

another family member to do the job; go shopping with Mom or Dad without having a tantrum or stay home with a baby-sitter.

4. *My clearly stated rule is* . . . The rule you state must have clear directions that include how, when, where, and how often. If what you want does not give a choice, such as "Feed the dog now" (versus "Feed the dog or we'll give him your dinner") then this is a "must behavior." When you demand that the child feed the dog you are willing to do whatever it takes to see that the job is done. This may mean taking the child by the hand to make sure the dog gets his food.

5. *The consequences are* . . . Ask yourself, "Can I live with the consequences that my child may experience when I give him choices?" "Feed the dog or we'll give him away" certainly draws the battle lines. "Please take a shower or your only friends will be the flies" leaves your child with the consequences of uncleanliness. Can you live with that? If so, it is a great teaching lesson, but one that affects you too.

6. *My follow-through will be* . . . Your rules will be either mandatory or optional. Either the child *must* do them or is given the *choice* to do them. Your response to what you set up brings us back to the concept of conditioning. Either you respond unpredictably like a slot machine (and thereby teach your kids to "play the odds") or else you respond the same way every time until they get the message. Arguing, procrastinating, forgetting, changing the subject, lying, and pitting one parent against the other are tactics that children use to foil your follow-through.

7. *Will I be consistent, no matter what it takes?* Inconsistency breeds manipulation, and manipulation

produces anger. Both the rules you choose for mandatory behaviors and those for which you give the freedom to choose must be consistently followed through. This is the biggest obstacle that parents face. Your kids will do everything in their power to get you to be inconsistent! Consistently enforce your rules and don't give children the option to misbehave.

With the seven decisions in mind, let's look at some common areas of conflict.

## The Messy Bedroom

Getting kids to do household chores is almost always a headache. As parents we somehow have the fantasy that our children should want to do the work because they are happy to be part of our family and because they love us so much ("If you don't do it that means you don't love me").

The fact is that no one I know likes to take out the trash, clean up dog messes, wash dishes, make beds, clean toilets, fold laundry or vacuum the carpet. We need to recognize the difference between doing chores and liking to do chores.

Let's take an example and walk through the seven steps for an 11-year-old boy. The problem is that the boy will not clean his room. All the nagging, pleading, and begging has not worked. The parents typically give up and do it themselves, scream until it is done, or just stop asking at all. In any case, the boy has learned through reinforcement that he does not have to clean the room every time or at all.

- *The behavior I want* is for the child to clean his bedroom. A clean bedroom means no clothes on the floor, the bed made to my satisfaction, dirty clothes in the hamper, a vacuumed floor, dusted furniture, and no food in the room overnight.

- *I might be feeding the behavior I do not want* by nagging him to make his bed at the wrong time, picking up his dirty clothes for him, letting him take dessert to his room, and forgetting to tell him to clean up his room at a certain time each day. I might also have the faulty belief that he cannot be responsible for cleaning up his room because he is in a stage of growth that does not permit him to make beds and pick up dirty clothes. Or maybe I believe he inherited his irresponsibility from his father and grandfather.

- *I will give him several choices.* He may choose, with my okay, what day and time to dust and vacuum the room. The bed is to be made and the dirty clothes picked up each day by 7:15 A.M. on schooldays, and 10:00 A.M. on weekends. If he chooses not to complete the chores, then consequences will follow (as stated below).

- *My clearly stated rule is:* "You are to make your bed and pick up your dirty clothes and put them in the hamper by 7:15 each school morning. You will dust and vacuum your room once per week at a day and time of your choosing."

- *The consequences of not completing these tasks will be:* 1) Wash your own clothes for five days when you have not put them in the hamper for one morning; 2) pay a fee of one dollar to have your bed made by Mom, Dad, or your sister each day you do not complete the job;

3) do not leave your room until the furniture is dusted and floor vacuumed on the day you have chosen to do it.

• *My follow-through will be* to see that the jobs are done according to the agreement. I will not do his laundry, and will charge him a bed-making fee. If he tries to sneak his laundry into the rest of the clothes, I will separate them and put them on his floor and add the statement, "You are to do your own laundry for five days." He will not leave his room until it is vacuumed and dusted on the day and by the time we have set in advance. If he leaves his room I will firmly escort him back and put the dust rag in his hand and say, "*When* you have finished the dusting and vacuuming, *then* you may come out."

• *I will be consistent* by not washing his clothes, even if he pleads, begs, and cries "child abuse." He will be charged every time for having someone else make his bed for him. I will also enforce the dusting and vacuuming by confining him to his room until it is done. If I am unwilling to be consistent in enforcing these rules, then I must live with giving him the option not to do them, and live instead with a messy room, dirty clothes, and ants in the room.

## Bedtime Blues

It can be a very pleasant experience to have the whole family in bed together. Unfortunately, this can turn into an every-night occurrence, with Mom and Dad having to fight for sleeping space and finding their five-year-old's foot in their faces when they wake up. When sleeping in Mommy's bed becomes a problem, parents often find it difficult to teach the child to stay in his own bed. Let's apply the seven steps to the "nighttime intruder."

- *The behavior I want* is that she stay in bed and sleep in her bed all night.
- *I might be feeding the problem* by inconsistently letting her sleep with us one night and insisting that she get back into bed the next night. She has learned to play the odds. I have also not been clear about the routine I want for her each night. She goes to bed at various times, sometimes having a story, other times forgetting to brush her teeth.

(You might ask yourself at this point if you somehow subtly encourage the child to sleep with you. Some couples with marital conflict purposely put the child between them to help keep a distance from each other. Others have a fear that the child will not feel loved and that they will be perceived as poor parents. These parents cannot "send" the child back to her bed.)

- *I will not give the child a choice of behavior; this is a "must."* My daughter is to get in bed and stay in bed all night. Special circumstances might be lightning-and-thunder storms, which can be very scary to her.
- *My clearly stated rule is:* "You are a big girl now. It is time for you to learn to stay in your own bed all night. When we have put you to bed and you get out and try to climb into our bed, I will take you back to your own bed every time."
- *The consequences will be* to put the child back into bed each time. For some children a two-minute "time

out" would work if you've found that works well for other misbehaviors. Each time she gets out of bed and comes into your room, you say, "That is two minutes of time out. I will set the timer." With younger children, gold stars work effectively. You could give her a gold star for every night she stays in bed. The gold star might mean that she gets 15 minutes of story time with Mom or Dad in her bed in the morning, or a special treat after breakfast, or 15 more minutes of TV. Whatever your child's interest, use it as a reward.

• *My follow-through will be* to walk her back to her bed each time she gets out. Or, if I use time out, I will walk her to the bathroom and set the timer for two minutes. When the time is up, I will walk her to her room and say, "You are not to get out of this bed again until morning."

• *I will be consistent in following through* each time my daughter gets out of bed. What is true today is true tomorrow. She will get a gold star in the morning whenever she stays in bed, or else be escorted by me to time out or directly back to bed. If I will not be consistent in enforcing this rule, then I will give the child the freedom to get out of bed whenever she wants to.

## Temper Tantrums

Most parents seem to have trouble with children who throw frequent temper tantrums. Telling the child that he cannot have or do something results in flailing arms, ear-piercing screams, hitting, running, and throwing things. The little nuclear explosion may last from a fortunate few minutes to as long as 30 or 40 minutes. These can happen several times a day, leaving a parent feeling like he's been through a war.

Kids seem to know when to have a tantrum—at the supermarket, when company is visiting, on the playground, or at a relative's house. It can get to the point where you are afraid to say no to the child—which is just where the child wants you! The basic idea is to teach the child that temper tantrums don't work. You must not let them "pay off." Let's walk through the seven decisions concerning temper tantrums, using an eight-year-old boy as an example.

- *The behavior I want changed* is for my son to react to a "No" without screaming, yelling, kicking, door-slamming, running away, or hitting.
- *I am feeding this behavior* by arguing with him, making it pay off through inconsistently giving in to quiet him down, taking him places after I had told him I would not because of his behavior, not following through on my discipline when I said I would, screaming at him and having a tantrum of my own, and believing that he could not control himself ("The devil makes him do it") or that "other kids do it" and therefore it is normal.
- *I will not give the child a choice.* I will not tolerate tantrums, nor will I reinforce them with a payoff by giving in. I will give the child a choice when it comes to going out in public. If he throws a tantrum, he will not go with me again until he has shown more control at home.
- *My clearly stated rule is:* "You are a big boy now and can do lots of things. One problem that worries your mother and me is that a lot of times when we say no, you get very upset and then yell, slam doors, throw things,

or fall on the floor kicking and screaming. We know you can stop this. We will not tolerate this kind of behavior anymore." When it happens again, say, "I want you to calm down now," "Quit throwing things now," or "Stop screaming now."

• *The consequences for throwing a tantrum will be* time out for two minutes. I will set the timer so he can hear it. When it goes off he can come out. If he does not go into the time out when he is told, it will be an extra minute for not obeying. If he is noisy when he is in TO, this will also result in an extra minute. He will clean up any mess he has made while in TO. If he throws a tantrum while at a neighbor's house or at the store, it will be TO when he gets home. To reinforce your child when he does comply, use a gold-star chart. Reward him with a gold star every time you say no and he doesn't have a fit.

Some children do not respond as well to time out as they do to your leaving the room. In that case, when the child throws a tantrum, leave the room (provided that he is not thrashing around breaking things). You can say, "Stop this screaming now or I will leave the room until you do." Remember, to have a fit you need an audience in order to get a payoff.

For older children who get violent and can cause harm to themselves or others, you must intervene. Remain calm, but do all you can to stop the tantrum. This may mean holding the child, sitting or lying on him, calling a neighbor for help, or even calling the police if necessary.

• *My follow-through will be* to remain calm and not to argue, scream, or yell back at the child. I will not let the

tantrum pay off. Each time the child has a
will send him to time out for two minutes or
the room until he has calmed down. If he is getting out
of hand, I will do whatever it takes to control him.

• *I will be consistent* by not giving in and letting the
child have his own way. I will use time out for every
tantrum. The child will not talk me out of it! If I am
unwilling to enforce this rule, I will give the child the
option to scream as much as he wants to.

## Fighting with Siblings

Without a doubt, fighting with siblings is on every
parent's "top ten" list. The reasons for fighting are as
different as the children themselves. Some kids need
space and the other sibling does not understand or
respect that need; other children are jealous of their
brother or sister (feeling that Mom and Dad have favor-
ites) and take out their hurt feelings in destructive
ways. Yet there is a certain degree of normality in
sibling fights. Having a need for one's own space and at
the same time recognizing the right of the other person
to his space is at the heart of this issue. The child who
enters Mom and Dad's room without knocking is not
respecting the rights of the parents. At the same time,
do Mom and Dad knock before entering the child's
room?

• *The behavior I want* is for the children to stop
fighting and to work the problems out themselves.

• *I might be feeding this problem* by yelling at them and
calling them names, thereby modeling the behavior I
want to extinguish. As a result, the problem escalates.

Or I could be inconsistently responding to tattling one time and ignoring it another, giving the children the message that sometimes it pays off. Maybe I favor one child over the other, and the fighting is a response of hurt feelings. It could also be that I do not respect their need for space, and so they don't understand or imitate this behavior with me. Or perhaps my kids lack experience in working things out in any way other than fighting and name-calling.

- *I will not give them a choice to fight* when they begin to call each other names, hit, kick, bite, take things from each other, or enter the other person's room without permission. Or you might feel that it is okay to fight and could say instead, *I will not give them the choice of fighting around me. I don't want to hear it.* Instead, when they come to me to tattle, I will ask them to work it out in another room.

- *My clearly stated rule is:* "Never hit each other, call each other names, enter bedrooms without permission, or take another person's possessions without first asking" or "Do not argue or fight in the house. I don't want to hear it, so do it outside in the yard or garage."

- *The consequences for fighting will be* that I will step in and break up the argument if it involves hitting or name-calling. I will not play judge and jury but will send each child to time out for three minutes. Or I will ask them what they intend to do about the problem and then send them to another part of the house to work it out. If I'm in the car I will pull over and demand that they stop the fighting.

If the children are young, between four and nine years old, you could set up a gold-star chart system whereby each child would get a gold star for each time you observe him playing well with other children. At the end of the day the stars would be added up and exchanged for something he might want, such as a special story from Dad, more time to play outside, a later bedtime, or a favorite candy. Another possibility would be to reinforce the older child every time he ignores, walks away from, or in some positive way settles the problem with his younger sibling. You are thereby strengthening his problem-solving skills with positive reinforcement.

• *My follow-through will be* to enforce the consequences I have set up in advance with my children. These will be clearly spelled out so they can reliably predict what my reaction will be—whether I send them to time out, tell them to go outside and work it out, or ask them what they intend to do about it without telling them how they should work it out.

• *I will be consistent* by following through with my plan every time I hear or see an argument. If I will not be consistent, then I might as well let them do as they please and live with the results.

## Failure to Do Homework

Keeping tabs on homework is tedious and difficult at best. Each kid seems to have a different definition of homework. "I did it in class" or "She didn't give us any" are common replies to a parent's inquiry. To some kids, when a teacher says "Read pages 50 to 60 by Friday," this doesn't qualify as homework. After all, there is really nothing to write or do—just read! And it can be done while watching TV or during lunch at school.

Homework, progress reports, Friday assignment sheets, and midquarter or semester grades all are important tools to indicate how well your child is doing. Yet the most-often-overlooked barometer is the teacher. It is imperative that you get the information from the horse's mouth. As a former teacher myself, I know how distorted my words and assignments got when they passed from my mouth through the youngster's to the parent. When in doubt, check it out! Find out how much homework is typical per day or week, how often quizzes and tests are given, when reports or projects will be due during the quarter, and what the procedure is for getting a weekly progress report. Don't overlook this valuable source of information. You may feel that the teachers don't want to be bothered by you, but it is your child's education that is at stake.

•   *The behavior I want* is for my child to do every homework assignment and to turn it in on time. I want to see the work when it is completed. I also want a weekly report, signed by every teacher, telling me assignments missed, classroom behavior, and current grade.

•   *I might be feeding the problem* by not requiring my child to do the homework, being unaware of assignments due, having no knowledge of the teacher's requirements, giving up, or having a lack of follow-through in checking up on homework completions. Some children do homework like clockwork. For others, it's akin to going to the dentist. If you have a child with problems in school that are not related to a learning disability, then you are probably guilty of one of the above behaviors.

- *I will not give them a choice* in doing homework. Just as I work and have responsibilities, so my children's responsibility is to go to school and get an education. When they are older (16 to 18), then they are responsible for their own work. If they do not wish to go to school, then they must begin to support themselves and pay rent.

- *My clearly stated rule is:* "Do every homework assignment, show it to me for corrections, and turn it in on time."

- *The consequences for not doing homework will be* restriction to the house until the homework is finished plus limited time watching TV, talking on the telephone, and listening to the radio. I will also hire a tutor for subjects that seem difficult for my child, have a quarterly conference with the teacher(s), and establish a weekly report system.

Younger children in elementary school can be set up on a gold-star chart system. Each time they complete their homework and show it to you for review, they receive a star. The stars can then be exchanged for something they want, such as more time to play, a snack, TV time, or points toward purchase of a valued toy.

- *My follow-through will be* to see that the homework is finished and the assignments turned in on time. I will see to it that homework is done about the same time each day. If I work, "homework time" is when I get home unless he has it done by the time I arrive so I may check it. If my child has inconsistently done his homework in the past, my presence may be necessary to insure that he does it. I will make sure that he studies in a quiet place that is well-lighted and has room to write. He will have no interruptions and no radio or TV. I will schedule teacher conferences when I am not sure of assignments.

• *I will be consistent* by following through every day to see that assignments are checked over and finished. If I do not want to do this, then I will give my child the option to do the homework if and when he wants to.

## Cutting Classes

As children grow into teenagers, the problem of cutting classes or cutting school altogether can become more of a problem. Often parents find out about such occurrences only after several instances. Kids get their friends to forge notes or call the school and impersonate their parents, or else they just don't show up, wandering off campus instead. If this goes unchecked, the young person learns that he doesn't have to stay in school and can leave whenever he wants to. This leads to unsupervised time and a high incidence of stealing and drug or alcohol use as well as a variety of delinquent behaviors.

• *The behavior I want* is that my child attend school every day and be in every class the whole time.
• *I might be feeding this problem* by not checking up on his school attendance when I notice that his grades are poor, believing him when he tells me he is attending but the school says he isn't, or letting him have a few days off every once in a while even though his grades are poor.

- *I will not give him a choice.* His primary responsibility is to get an education. He will attend school every day and will graduate. However, when he is older I may give him the option of no longer attending school but getting a job and paying for food and rent.
- *My clearly stated rule will be:* "Go to class every day and attend every class for the whole period. Never cut class or school again."
- *The consequences for cutting classes or school will be* that I drag him out of bed and accompany him to each and every class on the day after he has cut class or school. I will explain to the teachers in advance what I will be doing and will request a daily report from each teacher concerning his attendance.
- *My follow-through will be* to obtain teacher verification of his attendance and to take him to school and sit with him in class the day following his truancy.
- *I will be consistent* by following through to make sure he is in class the next day. If I am not willing to go all the way on this, then I will give him the freedom to attend or cut school as he pleases, or to drop out and pay rent.

### Curfew Problems

Some kids obey curfew times like clockwork while others forget every Saturday night what time they were supposed to be in. They use such excuses as "There were no phones so I couldn't call," "I wasn't driving so no one could bring me home," "We fell asleep," "The other car broke down," "I was with the church group so I thought it was okay," or "I forgot if you said 12:30 or 1:30."

A good rule of thumb is to give kids the amount of freedom that their behavior justifies. If your child has a history of not coming in on time or not telling you where he will be, then you need to keep him home, go get him, dock time off the next date, or go with him on the date! Each school year or birthday, *depending on previous behavior*, curfew times can be extended. As you work your way out of a job, the teenager will no longer need a curfew.

- *The behavior I want* is for my child to be home at the appointed time on school nights and on weekends.
- *I might be feeding this behavior* by not demanding he be in on time, changing curfew times, allowing excuses, or not checking up on him when he comes home.
- *I will not give him a choice* once we have set a curfew time. He must call me when he knows that he will not make it home at the time he said he would. Kids that ordinarily come in on time can be given the discretion to call if they are going to be late.
- *My clearly stated rule is:* "You are to be home at _____ tonight. That means inside the house at this time. On weekends the curfew is _____. This also means to be in the house by this time." (Kids often think that being home means sitting in the car out front or standing on the porch!)
- *The consequences will be* to restrict the teenager from going out the next time, to dock him the equivalent amount of time he was late from the next time he goes out, to call him on the telephone to tell him to come home, to go and get him, or to accompany him on his next date.

- *My follow-through will be* to be awake when my son or daughter comes home, or to set my alarm at the appointed time to see if she is in yet. If she is late, I will either restrict her from going out, dock time off on her next date, call her the next time she is late, or go on the date with her.

- *I will be consistent* in demanding that my child be home at the appointed time every time until he can begin to enforce the rule himself without needing an extra partner on his dates.

I hope this chapter gives you a blueprint to get back in control. You must know what you want and be able to communicate this information to your son or daughter in clear, precise terms. Your follow-through and consistency are vital to enforcing your position as a parent. As children grow, their behavior will dictate how much freedom you allow them. But first they need to know what you expect from them.

# 10

# Getting Back in Control

Let's be honest—some things are difficult to talk about with our kids. But have you ever thought how hard it might be for our children to talk to us? Healthy relationships are built on communication, both verbal and nonverbal. Your relationship with your children is shaped by how you communicate your attitudes, values, and beliefs about them. Effective communication is hard enough when you and your children are at peace, but it's that much harder to be patient and loving with a child when the two of you are constantly at war. It's especially difficult for a child to be loving and thoughtful when he hears belittling comments, sarcasm, yelling, and screaming, and receives discipline that is inconsistent, illogical, or vengeful.

## TURNING THINGS AROUND

You *can* turn things around. You are the parent, and it's your responsibility to act first. No matter how long you have battled, your kids can get the message that you want to have a better relationship. It's not necessary for them to want it first. You may have to reach out and pull them back into the family with the tenacity of a bulldog, whether they want you to or not. It can be done. Let's look at how you can begin to do this.

### Communicate

There's an axiom in communication theory that says *"You cannot not communicate."* In other words, all that you do and say communicates something to those around you. How many times we've heard a wife complain that her husband hides behind the newspaper as she asks him about his day! His message is clear: "Leave me alone. I don't want to talk." The teenager who goes in his room and keeps the door closed is giving a message: "Stay out. I need space." He may or may not be angry; he might just need some valued time alone. When a daughter comes home after school, slams the door, and heaves a big sigh, she too is saying something about her feelings.

One research study by Dr. A. Mehrabín, reported in his book *Silent Messages*, demonstrated that the loudest messages are nonverbal: 55 percent of what we communicate consists of nonverbal messages sent through eye contact (or lack of eye contact), facial expressions, and body language; 38 percent is tone of voice (how we say what we say), and *only 7 percent* is content! So the mother who washes dishes as her daughter tells what happened at school that day is sending a message: "I'm more interested in washing dishes than in focusing all my attention on you." The dad who talks to the kids only while he's watching TV is also conveying a clear message: "I'm more interested in my TV show than in what you have to say."

Examine how you nonverbally communicate with your children. Are you always busy when they talk to you? Do they feel they must compete with a pot of spaghetti? Are your kids standing in front of the TV set to get your attention? If you absolutely cannot give them your full attention, then it is important to say, "Now is not a good time for me to listen to what you have to say. I want to give you my full attention, but I can't right now. Can we talk after dinner at 7:30?" Kids need to be aware of Mom and Dad's needs as well. So if you say "later," make sure that later does come.

If your children are small, *talk to them at eye level.* I once stood next to former professional basketball star Wilt Chamberlain. When I looked up at him, I felt like a little kid. I gained a new understanding of what it's like for our little ones to look up to us. They feel pretty small. Wilt understands this so well that his house has several levels of floors so that people of different heights can stand and talk to him eye-to-eye!

Another key to reviving your relationships with your kids is to become an empathetic listener and responder. This means stepping outside yourself to share or experience the feelings of another person. I think many parents understand what their child is going through, but they fail to empathize with the child so he knows that Mom and Dad understand. Statements of blame such as "It's your fault, now go fix it," labels such as "You're so selfish," threats like "One more time and you'll get it," lectures such as "How many times do I have to tell you?" judgments like "That's an immature thing to say," and general statements like "All kids feel like this" are not empathetic responses but sure-fire resentment-builders.

Empathetic responses communicate that the youngster's thoughts and feelings count and are valuable. This does *not* give them permission to do whatever they want to, but it does allow them to feel what they feel and know that they are understood. Empathy communicates "Your feelings, wants, and values are important to me. I will not discount them in making my decision, even though that decision may not be what you want."

The following are examples of empathetic messages: "I can understand how extremely angry you are at me"; "It must really hurt a lot when something like that happens"; and "The frown on your face seems to say you don't like what I just said." Those statements communicate acceptance. They're a way of saying, "I think I know what you're feeling and I understand why you feel this way." Unfortunately, many of us believe that if we accept what a child or teenager feels and thinks, he will remain the way he is. Parents think, "If I agree that he is feeling a certain way, it's the same thing as giving him permission to do what he wants." Therefore we conclude that the best way to change someone is to tell him what we don't accept. But it is only when children know that you respect and accept who they are that they will have the freedom to risk making changes.

Remember: *Never argue with your child's feelings.* You can dispute facts, but you cannot get inside a person and tell him he can't feel the way he does!

Another way to begin to communicate with your child is to state *what you observe from his behavior:* "Kent, you aren't talking tonight at dinner. Is something wrong?" or "Tiffany, I noticed that when you came in from school today you went right to your room instead of saying 'Hi.' Are you okay?" Noticing a frown, a sad look, a slammed door, not eating dinner, and walking slower than usual are things you can mention to your child. In this way he gets the message that you are concerned, even if he doesn't tell you what's going on. A common complaint from teenagers is "My parents don't seem to care about what's happening to me." When you pick up on subtle and not-so-subtle changes in behavior, you can begin to correct this complaint and help your child sense that you really do care.

In addition to letting our children know we understand, empathetic messages help let off emotional steam and allow the child or teenager to think through an upsetting problem. When you or I experience intense emotions, we tend to lose perspective. When someone helps us think out loud about a problem, it helps us begin to solve the difficulty. Many of my clients in therapy ask, "Is what I'm feeling normal? Do other people feel like I do?" I assure them that they are not alone. This begins to free them from the emotional lock of isolation and allows them to explore the causes and solutions to their problems.

At the beginning of the school year my son wanted a "Pound Puppy" lunchbox. When we got to the store, and after pacing back and forth in front of the lunchbox display agonizing over the decision, he chose another kind. "David, you said you really wanted the 'Pound Puppy' lunchbox. What made you change your mind and choose this one?"

"I don't know," he answered. "I think it's because the kids at school will laugh at me."

"You think they'll make fun of you and you'll feel bad," I responded.

"Uh-huh."

"In that case maybe you'd like to wait until school starts and then decide," I suggested.

"Yeah, that's a good idea." Had I not responded in an understanding way, he might not have thought to wait and see, but would have picked a lunchbox that he really didn't want.

When you think about it, a good friend or marriage partner is one who can listen empathetically and "walk a mile in your shoes." My job as a psychologist and marriage and family counselor is to listen with as much understanding as I can, then to communicate this to my clients as we work together to solve their difficulties. I am continually amazed at how few people have someone who can do this with them. Many adults lacked parents who were able to empathize with their thoughts and feelings.

Encouraging one-word responses such as "Wow!" "Oh?" and "Really!" invites the youngster to share his ideas and feelings. These say "Keep talking; I'm available and interested." Door openers like "Tell me more about it," "This really seems important to you," "I'd like to hear all about it," and "Would you like to talk about it?" can also begin to get the conversation rolling. Your kids may not jump right in with excitement to these responses, but at least they know you are available and concerned.

Another communication skill is to *help kids give their feelings a name.* One of my specific objectives when working with people is to help them label their feelings. Not only do they see that I understand them when I do this, but it gives them a sense of control when they can pinpoint what they feel. We can do the same thing as parents. If a child says, "I went to every friend's house I know, and nobody can play," instead of responding "Well, it looks like you'll have to learn to play by yourself," you could say, "It's disappointing when there's no one to do things with." If a teenager says, "I just found out that my best friend, John, is moving away," instead of saying, "You'll make more friends; there's lots out there," you could say, "I'll bet you're shocked. To have a best friend move away really hurts."

*Communicate with your kids.* Listen, both verbally and nonverbally. Agree that their feelings are right *for them.* Let them know that they count and that they make a difference in your life. Give them eye contact, time together, and words of encouragement. Get rid of labels, accusations, and put-downs. Don't wait for them to do this for you. You're the parent; you must do it first!

Isn't this like our relationship with God? Some people feel that He is the big policeman in the sky, or the hovering parent marking off points for our every wrong, or maybe the detached spectator who doesn't see the subtle changes in our lives. That's no incentive to change and be better—only an incentive not to get caught doing wrong things. Instead, our heavenly Father desires us to be like Jesus. God has told us in the Bible that He loves us and wants the best for our lives. He has also demonstrated through His Son, Jesus, His complete love and commitment to us.

## Show Respect

Comedian Rodney Dangerfield has made a career out of "getting no respect." From the way people laugh and react to him, I'd say we all understand what he is talking about. Here are some statements I've heard from teenagers who feel like Rodney:

> "My father knocks and walks into my room all the time," said 15-year-old Jim. "He seems to think that as long as he knocks it's okay to come right on in. If I did that to him, he'd have a fit."
>
> "I hate it when my parents listen to my phone conversations," said 14-year-old Nicole. "They seem to swarm around me when I want to talk. Then they'll pick up the phone and tell me it's time to get off. I get so embarrassed!"
>
> "My mom likes to throw out things of mine," complained 17-year-old Steve. "It's as if she knows what needs to go and what needs

to stay. There are certain things I like to keep. It's not right for her to just throw my stuff away without asking first."

"What makes me angry is that my dad will never say that he's wrong and I'm right," said 16-year-old Sharon. "He always has to be right. Just once I'd like him to let me know that I'm right."

Respect is difficult to define. It has to do with a basic sense of value to one's self and to the other person. The common thread in all the statements that these young people made is "We don't feel that our needs, wants, and wishes are valued. Our parents demand that we respect *them* but when do *we* get respect?"

As parents, we will get respect when we give it. It begins in the first few years of life. From that first "no" to "I want privacy when I'm in the bathroom," children learn what it is like to have their needs and wants validated or ignored. If you think about it, God has the highest respect for our freedom—so much so that He has given us the freedom to choose Him or not. He doesn't want robots loving and praising Him; instead, He wants people who lovingly respond to His message of salvation.

So how do we begin to show our kids that we respect them? One way is in the area we've just looked at: communication—letting them know that we value what they think and feel. Again, this is not giving approval; it is respecting a child or teenager as a separate and distinct person. If some of the statements the teenagers said earlier hit home with you, and you want to show your children more respect, then begin by telling them something like "I've been reading this book on being a better parent. I realize that I don't always listen to you or give you my full attention. Sometimes I come into your room without knocking. I know how mad that makes you. I don't want to ignore your feelings. I'd like you to help me change."

Another way to show children and teenagers respect is to acknowledge their sense of a separate self. We can do this by allowing them to say no. When we hear that word from our kids, we often feel hurt, angry, pushed away, inadequate, bad, or defeated. Yet kids are simply telling us that they have a need which we discount when we ignore their "no." I'm not saying that we must agree with their "no," but we can at least acknowledge their feelings. Privacy in their rooms, visiting relatives, eating certain foods, wearing particular styles of clothing, and playing with certain friends are all areas in which kids tend to say no. You have to decide when it's necessary to override the "no." *Pick your battles wisely!* The older kids get, the more important it is to have few battlegrounds and therefore fewer "no's." The battlegrounds you do choose must be the most important ones, such as school attendance, use of alcohol and drugs, clothes and music, household jobs, curfews, and knowledge of their whereabouts.

Sometimes we can communicate respect by *nonintervention*. By doing nothing in a situation we can communicate trust. Keeping our hands off and mouths shut while a child or teenager is engaged in an activity, project, or relationship lets him know that we respect his right to handle things on his own. For example, you hear your 12-year-old son arguing with his best friend. Part of you wants to step in and referee, but the other part says, "Let them work it out." You must ask yourself, "If I step in, what will my son learn? On the other hand, what can he learn if I leave him alone?" Frequently, when we as parents interfere, intrude, check in, or correct, we invade a child's sense of self. We are telling him that he must do it our way and cannot do it alone. That undermines his self-confidence. Instead, we must work toward always treating our children as if they are capable. They view themselves in the way they think others see them. We have to allow our children and teenagers a measured degree of separateness as a way of saying, "I believe you are capable."

Another area in which it is extremely difficult for parents to allow a teenager different viewpoints and feelings is God and religion. The adolescent years are a time for trying on new "hats" or identities. As teenagers develop and mature, they become more idealistic and critical. Their attitudes toward parents, school, government, and God often suffer as a result. Fortunately, kids don't often put their action where their idealistic mouths are. They feel that if they protest something, it's the same as taking the energy to change it. As your teens question you about God, give them the freedom to explore who He is. "I don't think I believe in God anymore," one youngster might say. You could respond by saying, "It seems that you have some questions about whether He is real or not. What makes you wonder about Him?" This statement says that it's okay to ask questions and explore. That's how we come to know God and develop a conviction about our personal faith in God and Jesus Christ. Also, we often get asked questions to which we honestly don't know the answers. Don't bluff. Be straight with your teenagers and tell them you don't know, then try to find the answers together.

Jane Norman and Myron Harris in their book *The Private Life of the American Teenager* (Rowson, Wade, 1981) discuss several areas in which kids have said their parents could show more respect. In polling 160,000 teenagers from ages 13 to 18, they found that teenagers resent parents who:

- Reprimand them in front of their friends. Some kids don't want praise in front of their friends either!
- Treat them like babies.
- Pry into friends' lives. Young people resent parents who intrude.
- Continually initiate conversations about private matters. This too feels like prying.
- Expect them to tell their parents everything.
- Do not let them have privacy for their phone conversations.
- Read diaries or open personal mail.
- Never admit they are wrong.

It's true that when kids get into trouble with drugs or alcohol, at school or with the law, parents must intervene in direct ways. However, for the majority of children and teenagers the above findings must be heeded by us parents in order to let them know we respect them as individuals.

## Take Time for Fun

According to H. Stephen Glenn in his book *Developing Capable Young People,* in 1930 a child spent three to four hours a day personally involved with various members of the extended family. The extended family consisted of grandparents, aunts, uncles, and cousins, most of whom lived close by. Today's youngster lives with one or two parents plus other brothers and sisters. The grandparents, aunts, uncles, and cousins typically live far away. According to Glenn's statistics, interaction within modern-day families has been reduced to 14$\frac{1}{2}$ minutes per day! Of these minutes 12 are used in one-way negative communication in which parents shout out threats or scold children for wrongdoings. Based on these statistics, it doesn't sound like American families are having much fun together!

When I work with families, one of the questions I most often ask is "What do you do together to have fun?" When I asked one father this question he replied, "Why? What's the purpose?"

I almost fell out of my chair! "You feel that you must have a purpose to have fun with your kids?"

"Yes," he replied. "I've got a lot of things to do. We can talk and have fun while I'm working on the car in the garage." What is the message that his teenage boys were getting? "I will only spend time with you when I can be sure I'll get some things done. It will be only on my terms."

It's easy in our fast-paced society to neglect the vital "fun" aspect of family life. Yet our children and teenagers need to feel that we enjoy having fun with them and that we want to spend time with them.

Recently a couple brought their two teenage boys to see me. The 15-year-old wasn't doing well in school and the 12-year-old was beginning to slip in school as well. After discussing some problems in the family, I asked the older boy if his mom or dad ever talked to him about things other than school. He said they didn't.

"Do you and your dad ever do things together?" I asked.

"No," he replied.

At that point the mother gave the father a look that could kill. Based on that look I asked, "Is this also a problem in the family? Dad not having time with the boys?"

"Yes, it is," she responded. "I think it's a major problem."

We went on to talk about the father's experiences with his own dad. He said they rarely did things together. He felt inadequate, and didn't know how to do things with his teenage boys. So I gave the family a homework assignment to begin to correct this need: They were to come up with separate lists of things they would like to do together on a Father-Son day.

Each boy made a list, and so did Dad. The first day together, they decided to do something Dad liked (taking pictures) and something the boys liked (skateboarding). The idea was to have something enjoyable for everyone. The father taught the boys about photography and let them shoot some shots, and he took pictures of the boys skateboarding. When the family came back to see me, both the father and the sons were somewhat surprised that they could have fun together. This not only brought the men in the family closer together, but took Mom out of the position of being the family "nag." Now she could sit back and enjoy them having fun together.

Take time for fun! Dads, take your daughters on dates. Go shopping with them and let them teach you about current fashion. Take them to movies, and get dressed up and attend plays. Teach them how to change the oil in a car and balance the family checkbook. Moms, have your sons take you to ball games. Teach them how to cook, do laundry, plan family trips, and prepare a food budget. Use bedtime for talking with one another. Have family meetings to discuss financial matters, plan vacations, assign household jobs, and decide on weekend activities. Start doing these things now; it's never too late!

The focus of this book has been to help you examine the expectations you have of your kids. All of us parents need to decide what we want from our children. Remember, not deciding is also a decision. It tells children that they make the rules, that they are in control. Our children need a sense of security through knowing what is expected of them. Clearly stating what we want, following through, and consistently enforcing our rules are at the heart of regaining control of our parenting.

Above all, our children need to know that we value them as individuals. This means that we can enjoy them as separate persons, with their own wants, needs, and goals that may or may not be the same as ours. This freedom to be themselves also removes any need to rebel in order to become that separate being.

In closing this chapter, I would like to quote Dorothy Law Nolte as she summarizes how parents can model

communication, acceptance, respect, and enjoyment
of their children and teenagers:

> If a child lives with criticism,
>    He learns to condemn.
> If a child lives with hostility,
>    He learns to fight.
> If a child lives with ridicule,
>    He learns to be shy.
> If a child lives with shame,
>    He learns to feel guilty.
> If a child lives with tolerance,
>    He learns to be patient.
> If a child lives with encouragement,
>    He learns to be confident.
> If a child lives with praise,
>    He learns to appreciate.
> If a child lives with fairness,
>    He will learn justice.
> If a child lives with security,
>    He learns to have faith.
> If a child lives with approval,
>    He learns to like himself.
> If a child lives with acceptance and
>        friendship,
>    He learns to find love in the world.*

* Poem by Dorothy Law Nolte. Used by permission of *Upreach* maga-
zine, Abilene, Texas.